William Eleroy Curtis

The Yankees of the East

Sketches of modern Japan. Vol. 1

William Eleroy Curtis

The Yankees of the East
Sketches of modern Japan. Vol. 1

ISBN/EAN: 9783337097066

Printed in Europe, USA, Canada, Australia, Japan

Cover: Foto ©ninafisch / pixelio.de

More available books at **www.hansebooks.com**

THE YANKEES OF THE EAST

SKETCHES OF MODERN JAPAN

BY
WILLIAM ELEROY CURTIS

VOLUME I

NEW YORK
STONE & KIMBALL
MDCCCXCVI

TO
VICTOR F. LAWSON
THE PRINCE OF EMPLOYERS, THIS BOOK IS AFFECTIONATELY DEDICATED

CONTENTS

I. A WORD TO THE WISE	1
II. THE GOVERNMENT OF JAPAN	27
III. THE IMPERIAL FAMILY	61
IV. THE TYCOON IN SECLUSION	107
V. SOME SUGGESTIONS ABOUT SHOPPING	124
VI. THE FOREIGN COMMERCE OF JAPAN	138
VII. RAILWAYS AND 'RIKISHAS	168
VIII. THE POLICE, THE COURTS AND THE PRISONS	200
IX. MARRIAGE AND DIVORCE	233
X. JAPANESE JOURNALISM	268
XI. CONCERNING TRADE AND INVESTMENTS	293

List of Illustrations.

Volume I.

FUJAIMA, THE SACRED MOUNTAIN	*Frontispiece*
A JAPANESE TOMBSTONE	*To face page* 10
MARQUIS ITO, PRIME MINISTER	41
A JAPANESE RESIDENCE	59
THE PRINCE IMPÉRIAL	69
"THE BUND," YOKOHAMA	80
THE WALL OF THE IMPERIAL PALACE, TOKYO	98
GATEWAY TO THE IMPERIAL PALACE, TOKYO	103
APPROACH TO THE GREAT TEMPLES AT NIKKO	107
THE SACRED BRIDGE AT NIKKO	109
RECENT PORTRAIT OF THE EMPEROR	113
PAPPENBURG ISLAND, NAGASAKI HARBOR	116
A DRY-GOODS SHOP	124
THE GREAT CASTLE AT NAGOYA	130
THE OLD-FASHIONED WAY OF SPINNING	146
WRESTLERS READY TO SPRING	197
ENTRANCE TO THE SHRINE OF IEYASU, NIKKO	205
TOMB OF IEYASU, THE GREAT SHOGUN	211
MADAME CHRYSANTHEMUM AT HOME	233
THE OLD WAY	251
THE NEW WAY	253
THE NEW-FASHIONED WAY OF SPINNING — COTTON FACTORY AT OSAKA	276
A JAPANESE JUNK	297

The Yankees of the East

I

A Word to the Wise

That there may be no misunderstanding as to the motive of this contribution to the already voluminous literature concerning Japan, I will print the moral at the beginning instead of at the end of the story: which is to encourage every man, woman and child, twelve years old and upward, who have the time and money, to visit the land of fans and flowers before its original picturesqueness is entirely overcast with the commonplace and colorless customs of modern civilization.

The history of humankind does not furnish a stronger contrast than appears between the Japan upon which the sun of the nineteenth century rose, and the Japan upon which it sets. The great Tycoon, who ruled the empire with such splendor and arrogance, has fled for shelter to the old castle at Shizuoka, while upon the throne sits a wise, prudent and progressive emperor, who voluntarily surrendered the despotic power

The Yankees of the East

that had been exercised by his ancestors for twenty-five hundred years, and offered his subjects a constitution and a parliament. The daimyo, or feudal prince of ancient times, in his gorgeous robes of gold brocade, his jeweled swords and grotesque armor, has vanished; and in his place appears a very elegant and courteous gentleman, who plays polo and poker, and visits his club after dinner each evening in a piccadilly collar, a Tuxedo jacket and patent leather shoes, to read the periodicals from London and New York, and discuss the fluctuations in the rice and stock markets. The stately samurai, who used to commit suicide when he was insulted, has become the energetic man of affairs, who directs the political and financial policy of the empire from the cabinet offices and the parliament house, commands the army and the navy, edits the newspapers, superintends the schools, manages the railways and steamship lines, the banks and manufactories, and is guiding with great sagacity the social and industrial revolution that has possessed the people. A million images of Buddha have been shipped as bric-a-brac to Europe and America, and a law that makes education compulsory has brought three million children into free public schools and kindergartens, where they are given a thorough practical training, with modern text-books and scientific apparatus.

A Word to the Wise

Sunshine and joy may be found in every corner of this adorable old world, but they have not been evenly distributed. Japan has more than her share. No country on either hemisphere offers greater attractions to students and ordinary travelers, while to merchants and manufacturers it affords opportunities for trade and investment that do not exist elsewhere.

You can reach Japan from the United States by four steamship lines. That which connects with the Canadian Pacific railroad at Vancouver crosses the Pacific to Yokohama in twelve days, taking the northern route, which is cold, stormy and afflicted with frequent fogs; there are also steamers connecting with the Northern Pacific railroad at Tacoma, but they are slow, and not very comfortable for passengers. The Pacific Mail and the Oriental & Occidental steamers sail from San Francisco. They usually take from fourteen to sixteen days in making the voyage, and every other steamer, which touches at Honolulu, requires twenty days; but the latter is by far the most agreeable and attractive route, because you are always pretty sure of getting good weather and a smooth sea.

The Grand hotel at Yokohama stands at the gateway of the east, and its long balcony faces the rising sun. There one can observe everything that enters and everything that leaves Japan, and a tide of people is ebbing and flowing in-

The Yankees of the East

cessantly with the arrival and departure of the steamers that furnish communication with the four quarters of the earth. Upon that balcony are samples of the citizenship of every civilized nation, mingling their dialects with the music of a native band that plays Sousa's popular music, and is always required to repeat the "Liberty Bell," the "Washington Post March," and other familiar numbers.

The infallible Britons, usually the most numerous, have been able to fix the etiquette and the habits of the place. They have fastened their accent and their idioms upon the common vocabulary. Their commercial travelers are forever in evidence, while representatives of American manufacturers are few and far between. The newspaper fraternity is represented by correspondents of English, French and American papers. There are usually several naval officers bound outward to join their ships or homeward after a cruise in the Asiatic seas, and diplomatists en route to or from their stations. The wives of the navies of all nations make their temporary home there while their husbands are in the east, because of the social attractions and the convenient location of Yokohama; and several people with money and leisure live there continually because they like the climate and the customs of Japan.

But the names upon the register of the Grand

A Word to the Wise

hotel are mostly those of tourists, globe-trotters and curio buyers from England and America, and some of them are queer folk. As a young lady of limited experience remarked, "It does seem as if all the odd people in the world were traveling." You seldom miss Galusha Ruggles, who asserts his Americanism on every occasion, or Miss Lincrusta Walton, who is chaperoned by his self-reliant wife. Lord Deliverus, with his broad a's and large feet, always occupies a great deal of attention; a French marquis with vehement gestures and incessant chatter sits at the next table, and just beyond him is a Russian boyar with big rings and ill-fitting garments. The Germans are clannish, and cling together, and along toward the end of the dinner hour you hear "Hoch!" "Hoch!" as they drink to the Fatherland. The Hindoos wear combs in their blue-black hair, and rings in their ears. The Chinese mandarins are robed in the finest texture and the most delicate shades of silk. The orthodox evening dress for summer is a white suit of duck much like those worn by the cadets at West Point and Annapolis, with the jacket cut very short and a plaited belt of black, blue or scarlet silk. Their shoes are of white canvas, chalked with great care, while the duck is starched so stiff as to look very uncomfortable.

Three months and $1,000 are sufficient to see

The Yankees of the East

Japan if you are able to resist the temptation to buy silks and bric-a-brac. It is not necessary to go everywhere. A few days in Yokohama; a week or two in Tokyo, which is only eighteen miles distant, and abounds in interests; a pilgrimage to the betempled groves of Nikko, which is three or four hours by rail from the capital; a few days at Miyanoshita, a famous summer resort on the breast of Fujiyama, the sacred mountain; thence by rail to Kyoto, the ancient capital, a journey of fifteen hours, where one or two weeks can be spent profitably; a side trip to Nara, a hallowed spot to believers in Buddhism; a week in Osaka, which is the Chicago of Japan, a miracle of progress and industry; and a day or two at Kobe, the central seaport, will give one a very fair idea of ancient and modern Japan. Then at Kobe the traveler should take a steamer through the inland sea, which is beautiful but has been over-praised, to Nagasaki, the farther end of the empire. From there the steamers sail for China, India and Europe, and a trip to Shanghai would be profitable.

There is a good deal of competition in freights between the United States and Japan. Two new steamship lines have recently started with the expectation of a boom in trade, and another is promised. For nearly thirty-five years the Pacific Mail Steamship company had a monopoly of the business. Then, when the Canadian

A Word to the Wise

Pacific railroad was finished that corporation put on what is known as the Empress line. There was a fight at first for cargoes, but the two companies finally reconciled matters and found there was freight enough for both at good rates. Then the Central Pacific railroad chartered four vessels that had been operated by the White Star company on the transatlantic line, put new engines into them and modern improvements, and has been running them with profit. More recently the Northern Pacific company, in anticipation of the increased trade that everybody thinks is coming, chartered some of the old Cunard ships, and is operating them under new names. The Oregon Railway and Navigation company has also entered into competition for some of the business, with steamers chartered from a London company, which have been running to Hong Kong and Shanghai, and the Great Northern railway, sooner or later, will put on a fleet. President Hill was about to let contracts for three beautiful ships when the hard times set in about two years ago, and reluctantly postponed the work until financial affairs are brighter.

It costs about $40,000 to take a first-class passenger ship across the Pacific and back, the cost increasing rapidly with the speed, as coal is the chief item. It needs twice as much coal to drive the same ship at a speed of fifteen knots

The Yankees of the East

an hour as would be required for ten knots. That is the reason the Pacific Mail company declined a government subsidy. The law required them to make fifteen knots an hour, but the pay was only $1 a mile one way, or about $5,600 for the voyage, which would not cover the additional expense for fuel. It costs more to make a voyage to Japan than to come home, because coal is $7 a ton in San Francisco, while it is only $2 and $2.25 in Japan.

Most of the outward freight is flour. Most of the return freight is raw silk, tea, opium and rice. The latter is taken for ballast when necessary. Most of the tea goes to Chicago; most of the silk to Paterson, N. J., and to Providence, R. I. The rice is all consigned to San Francisco.

The shipments of flour are increasing rapidly with low prices. There were 16,000 barrels in the hold of the steamer in which I sailed and it usually makes up nine-tenths of the cargo. The steamers carry little machinery as freight—only now and then a rice-crushing machine or some railroad supplies. It is not referred to upon the printed freight schedules, but special rates are made when it is offered—at $8 or $10 a ton, according to the cubic space occupied. Heavy shipments of machinery are made in sailing vessels.

Opium is the most profitable freight, and large amounts are brought in on nearly every

A Word to the Wise

steamer to San Francisco. The shipments are increasing and have almost doubled since the duty was reduced from $12 to $6 a pound. Part of this increase is due to the suppression of smuggling, but as the number of Chinese in the United States is decreasing, it is evident that the consumption is extending among other classes of people. The freight rate on opium is $8 a box, or $160 a ton. It comes from Macao, a Portuguese settlement opposite Hong Kong, as the Chinese government does not permit it to be exported from its ports. Nor are Chinamen allowed to import opium into the United States, so it is all consigned to a certain banking firm in San Francisco which is supposed to be acting for the Six Companies in that city.

Another curious freight shipped exclusively from San Francisco to China is "fish bones," which pays $20 a ton. It is sent in large boxes consigned to the Tung Wah hospital at Hong Kong, but the boxes really contain the bodies of dead Chinamen sent home for burial. Most of the coolies who come to the United States are under the care of the Six Companies, who sign a contract guaranteeing to return the bones of the dead for burial with their ancestors in the celestial empire, and the Tung Wah hospital acts as their agent in carrying out the agreement. They are shipped as "fish bones" in order to evade the rule of the steamship companies that im-

The Yankees of the East

poses full first-class passenger rates for the bodies of the dead.

Nearly every ship leaving San Francisco for China carries among the steerage passengers a number of invalids who hope to live until they reach their native country, but several usually die on every voyage. There is an agreement between the steamships and the Six Companies which forbids the burial of these bodies at sea, and the latter provides coffins of the peculiar Chinese pattern for use in such emergencies. They are made of slabs, the first cut of the log, so that the sides and bottom and top are rounded. A dozen or more are carried on each ship and the surgeon is furnished with a supply of embalming fluid.

When a Chinaman dies at sea the surgeon embalms the body, which is then placed in a coffin, sealed up and lowered into the hold. The expense is paid by voluntary contributions from the other Chinese passengers, the crew and the stewards of the ship, all of whom belong to that race. No subscription paper is passed around, but a pan containing Chinese sugar is placed beside the coffin. Every Chinaman on board drops in his contribution, from a dime to a dollar, and takes a piece of sugar from the pan, which is supposed to bring him good luck and prolong his life. When the ship reaches Hong Kong the coffins and the belongings of the

A JAPANESE TOMBSTONE.

A Word to the Wise

dead are delivered to the Tung Wah hospital, which disposes of them to the surviving friends in China. Every Chinaman in the United States is supposed to be registered at the Tung Wah hospital and with the Six Companies at San Francisco.

The officers of the Pacific Mail steamships say that Chinamen make the best sailors and servants on board ship of any race in the world. They never strike, they never complain, and if any one of them wants a day off he always supplies a substitute at his own expense. Most of the crews have been on the steamers continuously ever since they started—some of them for twenty years. They are honest and careful and save their money, which they send to their families in San Francisco or China as often as they are paid. Some of them have business ashore and are worth considerable property. Ah Mon, a dining-room boy on the steamer City of Rio de Janeiro, has a ranch near San Francisco, where his wife raises vegetables for market. Chee Sigh has a little shop in Hong Kong. Ah Pat has a wife at Feechau, two days' journey from Canton, to whom he sends all his wages. Ah Ting, the engineer's boy, has a frozen smile—a face like those upon the statues of Buddha—and a wife near Canton whom he hasn't seen for five years, but he sends her his wages every pay-day, and she is keeping the money for his old age. Ting

The Yankees of the East

has been with the ship ever since it has been running and has not missed a voyage. Once the company decided to dispense with Chinese servants and substitute Japanese. All the China boys were discharged, but Ting would not go. They drove him off the vessel twice and thought they had got rid of him, but the next morning after sailing the steward found him in the pantry washing dishes and he has been there ever since.

In crossing to Japan the Pacific Mail steamers pass very near the island that is celebrated as the scene of the adventures of those intrepid navigators, Mrs. Aleshine and Mrs. Lecks, in Frank R. Stockton's novel. It is a coral formation of recent date and known on the map as Midway island, or Brooks' island, having been discovered by Captain Brooks of the United States steamship Cambria as late as 1859. It is about seven miles long and two miles wide and almost entirely barren, although there has sprung up of late years a growth of low brush from seeds probably brought there by the birds. There are several pretty bays protected by coral reefs, but the bottom of the sea in that neighborhood is constantly changing because of subterranean disturbances and the industry of coral insects, so that navigation is dangerous. Captain Brooks took possession of the island in the name of the United States, and the Pacific Mail company established a depot there, with a store of

A Word to the Wise

coal and other supplies for the benefit of distressed vessels. A house was built and a Kamchatkan left in charge as custodian, but he became tired of his lonely life and ran away at the first opportunity. A log-book was placed in the house and visiting skippers were requested to register their names and vessels, but the hospitality it offered was abused by whalers who stopped on their way to the North Pacific. They not only helped themselves to the coal and provisions, but even tore down the house and used the timbers for fuel. A few years ago an American man-of-war visited the place and found it stripped of everything movable.

The Peninsular and Oriental Steam Navigation company of London, which is said to have the largest fleet of ships of any company in the world, furnishes communication with Great Britain via the Suez canal, stopping at the intermediate ports of China, India, Turkey and Egypt, with a heavy subsidy from the British government.

The French government subsidizes the steamers of the Compagnie des Messagaries Maritimes, which also connects with Chinese and Indian ports, and the German government the Norddeutscher Lloyd, which follows practically the same route to Hamburg, although the French steamers go only as far as Marseilles.

The voyage between Japan and San Fran-

The Yankees of the East

cisco is from fourteen to twenty days; to Tacoma and Portland, from twenty to twenty-five days; to Vancouver, from twelve to fourteen days; to London, from forty to forty-five days; to Marseilles, from thirty-five to forty days, and to Hamburg, from forty-five to fifty days. The passenger steamers of the American and Canadian lines sail once in three weeks, the English and French once in two weeks and the Germans once in four weeks.

There are also a number of British steamers sailing more or less regularly during the seasons when there is the greatest demand for freights. They carry no passengers, but keep down rates by affording competition with the regularly established companies. They have no regular routes, but go wherever it pays them, and often make voyages to New York. It is not difficult at any time during the silk and the tea season to find a through steamer to New York by the Suez canal with rates of freight very much lower than those charged by way of San Francisco. The Lambert & Holt company of London have steamers all the while loading for ports in all parts of the world, and carrying freights at rates that are amazingly low. Their vessels are especially built for such trade. They cost little for construction, have unusually large cargo space, make slow time with little fuel and are managed with great skill and economy, so that,

A Word to the Wise

as is often said, it costs no more to sustain a Lambert & Holt steamer loaded and under steam at sea than when lying empty in port.

Freights to Europe are comparatively cheaper than to the United States. The average rate a ton on merchandise to London is 35 shillings, or $8.75 a ton, while the lowest rate from San Francisco is $6 a ton. Freight is calculated either by cubic feet or weight, according to the option of the steamship company. If the goods are heavy they charge by weight. If they are light they charge by cubic feet, and a package about as large as an upright piano will be reckoned as a ton.

The freight to Marseilles and neighboring ports by the French line of steamers is about 30 shillings a ton, and to and from Hamburg about 40 shillings. These rates, given by the regular lines of steamers, can be made much cheaper by tramps if one offers a sufficient amount of cargo. The rate by sail to and from New York and other Atlantic ports via Cape Horn or the Cape of Good Hope will average about $8 a ton, and all heavy goods like iron and machinery from the eastern part of the United States are sent in that way because of the long railway haul across the continent. The British exporter can usually get his goods to the markets of Japan 30 or 40 per cent cheaper than the producer in Chicago, Pittsburg and other points in the interior of the

The Yankees of the East

United States, although the establishment of the new lines of steamers has had a decided tendency to reduce rates.

Japan has an area of nearly 150,000 square miles. It is about the size of Great Britain and Ireland, or the two Dakotas, and has a population of 41,089,940, including 20,752,336 males, 20,337,574 females and perhaps 20,000 savages in the northern islands that are not enumerated. Adding Formosa, that rich island that was acquired by the recent war, there are no less than 45,000,000 people under the Mikado's authority. The island is about the dimensions of Spain, and the new province makes Japan the eleventh country in Christendom in area, and the fifth in population. The density of population, particularly in the southern portions of the main island, is very great, about forty-nine to the square mile.

The death rate in 1894 was 2.27 per 100 of population and the birth rate 2.85. The total number of deaths was 937,644 and the total number of births 1,178,428, which indicates that the diet of the people and their constant labor does not seriously affect their health.

Tokyo is the largest city in the empire, and there the traveler can see modern Japan at its best. Yokohama is too foreign. Osaka will give the most correct glimpse of the Japan of the future, for it has made more rapid progress than

A Word to the Wise

any other place, and is to be the future center of the manufacturing industries. At Kyoto you can see old Japan to good advantage, and within a few miles of that, the ancient capital, are some most interesting excursions. A visit to Lake Biwa, a journey on a canal that runs under a mountain through a great tunnel, and a rush down the rapids of the Katsuragawa river, should by no means be omitted. They furnish an experience that will never be forgotten. Kyoto is the best place to do shopping, also. Prices are much lower there than in Yokohama or even Tokyo, and if you search the second-hand shops you can find glorious old temple hangings, embroidered brocades, and garments of rare design and great beauty that were worn a century ago. Don't buy anything in Yokohama until you return there after visiting other cities, or you will regret it. See the shops in Tokyo and Kyoto first. And you can get almost everything in New York or Chicago that the Yokohama merchants sell, although it will be fifty per cent cheaper in Japan.

When you visit Nikko take a journey by jinrikisha, or on horseback, to Lake Chuzenji and Yumoto, and see the most picturesque of Japanese scenery. And while at Miyanoshita do not fail to follow the mountain trails on foot or on ponyback wherever they lead.

At all these cities, and at the places I have

The Yankees of the East

named, there are excellent hotels, most of them kept on the American plan, and all of them furnishing good food and good beds. The stranger is always struck with the cleanliness of Japan. It is the neatest, cleanest country in the world. The people are splashing in the water and scrubbing their houses half the time, and there is scarcely a peasant or a beggar in all the empire who doesn't take a bath at least once a day.

The Japanese hotels are not comfortable for those who are accustomed to the luxury of modern travel in Europe and America, but there will be no complaint of their neatness or novelty. They contain no furniture whatever. Everybody eats and sleeps on the floor, and leaves his shoes in the vestibule. During the day you are given a mat or a cushion to sit upon and at night they spread a futon, which is a sort of comfortable, thickly padded with cotton, for your bed. The Japanese pillow is a block of wood, or an affair of woven strips of bamboo, five or six inches long and shaped like a small section of a railroad rail. This is placed under the neck as a man lies on his side or his back. It seems to have been originally invented in order to prevent the women from mussing up their hair—which is dressed in a skillful and wonderful manner by an artist who comes to the house about once a week—and is considered very comfortable by those who are accustomed to it;

A Word to the Wise

but an American who is in the habit of having a feather pillow under his head will dream that he is undergoing the extreme death penalty imposed by our courts of justice, and awaken in the morning with all the muscles in his neck protesting against a repetition of the experiment. It is well, therefore, for the traveler who goes into the interior, off the beaten line of travel, to carry in his rug roll a rubber pillow or a cushion that he can buy for seven or eight cents on any business street in any city.

The Japanese food does not satisfy the North American appetite, and an hour after one has finished a dinner he is hungrier than he was before. In most of the tea houses, which supply the place of hotels in the interior, you can have meat, fish and vegetables cooked after the American method, and your guide is usually capable of overseeing the undertaking, even if he cannot do it himself. It is always well, however, when one starts upon an expedition in the country, to secure a supply of canned soups and meats. The corn beef that is put up in Chicago has been the consolation of many hungry souls.

When a Japanese travels he has very little to consider, but if he is a pious Buddhist he usually goes to a temple and obtains from the priest who attends Jizu, the patron deity of travelers, a sealed packet, drawn by lot, which contains an omen that will indicate the result of his journey.

The Yankees of the East

Then he packs his cotton trunk, fastens it with a pin lock, and starts for the train. If he has any more baggage, it is placed in a curious looking basket and tied up with rope. If he is poor, he makes the journey on foot. Distances do not affect him.

Nature has given him perfect feet, that can spring him over fifty miles a day without pain; a stomach whose chemistry can extract ample nourishment from food on which no European could live; and a constitution that scorns heat, cold and damp alike, because it is still unimpaired by unhealthy clothing, by superfluous comforts, by the habit of seeking warmth from grates and stoves, and by wearing heavy leather shoes. If he desires to travel 1,000 miles he can get ready for his journey in five minutes. His whole outfit need not cost 75 cents, and all his baggage can be put into a handkerchief. On $10 he can travel for a year without work, or he can travel simply on his ability to work, or he can travel as a pilgrim.

The cost of living in a native hotel is very small. They will charge a foreigner one dollar a day, but a native seldom pays more than twenty-five cents. The prices at modern hotels are about what they are in the United States. In fact, the same degree of luxury and comfort costs about the same amount of money the world over, and a stranger is always expected to pay a

A Word to the Wise

heavy tax upon his ignorance and inexperience.

A great drawback to travel in the interior of Japan is the vigor and activity of the insect life. The natives, who are toughened by constant exposure, do not seem to notice it—although thirty, often ninety and sometimes ninety-nine per cent. of their skin is exposed to the air; so the tender flesh of foreigners is the more tempting, and, whenever one arrives in a rural town, the creeping and jumping things have a matsuri—that is the name of the Japanese festival when everybody comes out for a good time.

One hears of all sorts of remedies, as when he has the rheumatism or a bad cold. Flea powder, every possible variety of ointment, even sleeping bags are recommended, but none of them do any good. I have an intimate knowledge of beasts and birds of prey in other countries. They have a galley-nipper in Brazil and a bug in Bolivia which are said to carry tools around with them. They suck up all the poison in the atmosphere and inject it into your body with a sort of hypodermic pump. The Japanese insects are not so vicious, but are more active. They are always on the lookout for a job, and when night comes they commence business in earnest.

The people are cordial and hospitable. They overwhelm the traveler with attentions, and wherever you go make yourself known as an

The Yankees of the East

American. That is open sesame to every home and every heart in Japan. They hate the English, the French and the Russians, but treat them politely. That is due to their own self-respect and the laws of hospitality, but a citizen of the United States requires no further introduction than a mention of his nationality. The first question asked of a stranger is,

"O kuni wa?"—What is your honorable country?

And Englishmen who know the sentiments of the people often proclaim themselves Yankees in order to get the best rooms in the house, and the largest share of attention.

Every traveler should have a native guide or courier, who furnishes information on all subjects in the most eager manner. But that is his least useful attribute. The explanations and descriptions of the ordinary guide are weariness to the soul. But he is useful in finding places, in arranging routes of travel, in paying bills, and in shopping. In the latter alone he will save his wages, which are two yen, or one gold dollar, per day. He expects also to act as your valet, to wait upon you at the table, to brush your clothes, polish your boots, pack and unpack your trunk, and, when you get away from the American hotels, he buys your food and cooks your meals. He is altogether indispensable in these respects, but as interpreters most of the

A Word to the Wise

guides are awful, abominable and inexcusable humbugs. Renzo Sano is the best guide I found. He is a gentleman, a most agreeable companion and knows the country thoroughly.

The only trade union in Japan that attempts to regulate wages and hours of labor is the Kaiyusha, or Association of Guides, who have their regular fees, charges and printed rules, and are as arbitrary in dealing with their customers as any assembly of Knights of Labor in the United States. A tourist arriving in Japan must apply at headquarters if he wants a guide, and he gets the man whose name is first upon the list, regardless of any personal preference. This is often annoying, because some of the guides are competent and agreeable, while others are not. The only way to get a particular guide is to write several weeks in advance of your arrival and apply for him. Your letter is placed on file, and when his turn comes he is assigned to you, and whether you reach Japan before or after, his services and his pay commence on that date.

Murray has published a guide to Japan, but it is incomplete and unsatisfactory. The most useful books for the ordinary traveler are Chamberlain's "Things Japanese," and Miss Scidmore's "Jinrikisha Days." Griffis' "The Mikado's Empire," is the most satisfactory of all historical works. Dr. J. J. Rein's remarkable but costly volume is the best authority on the arts

The Yankees of the East

and industries of the country, and one can get the most accurate and comprehensive glimpse of Japanese home life by reading Miss Alice Bacon's "A Japanese Interior," and her "Japanese Girls and Women."

Sir Edwin Arnold's roseate views of Japan were obtained from a pretty villa at the top of a hill in the residence district of Tokyo, known as Azabu. It would not be polite or proper to repeat the gossip that is freely related concerning the behavior of this eminent gentleman during his stay in Japan, but it may be said that the missionaries do not refer to him as a shining example of morality. He wrote "The Light of Asia," at Omori, a popular seashore resort, where he was surrounded by a choice selection of geishi girls, and the guides now point out the scenes of his adventures as they do other places of historical interest.

The prose poems and pictures of Japanese life that have come from the pen of Lafcadio Hearn are a little more accurate than the writings of Sir Edwin, but practical people have not been able to see the same things in the same light as they appeared to his eyes. Mr. Hearn is a Greek by birth, and lived for many years in the United States, where he did newspaper work at Cincinnati and New Orleans. For a time he was a teacher in a government school in the interior of Japan, but later has been living in Kobe.

A Word to the Wise

He is a dreamer with a poetic temperament and a wonderful gift of words.

The usual word of greeting in Japan is "ohayo," which is pronounced "ohio," and they say that when John A. Bingham went over to be minister of the United States and everybody gave him this cordial welcome he expressed a great deal of gratification, but remarked sotto voce to a native acquaintance:

"How in thunder did all these people know I came from Ohio?"

Every Japanese is compelled to report at police headquarters whenever he changes his residence or his employer or his occupation. Whenever a man gets any kind of a job he is required to make it known to the officials, so that a perpetual census is being taken, and the police are supposed to know the name, residence, occupation and whereabouts of every person in the empire. All arrivals and departures at hotels and tea houses must be reported to the police. A complete record of births, deaths, marriages and divorces is kept also, and no native or stranger is allowed to leave the country, or even travel through it, without a passport.

The passports given to strangers and tourists are curious documents, being written in Japanese, with a translation in English. In accepting them tourists agree to observe certain regulations and are prohibited from doing some very

The Yankees of the East

ridiculous things. For example, one cannot travel at night in a carriage or jinrikisha without a light; he must not attend a fire on horseback, nor disregard notices of "No thoroughfare!" he must not drive rapidly upon narrow roadways, nor refuse to pay ferry and bridge tolls. He is prohibited from removing advertising signs from stores or houses or mileposts from the public highways. He must not break other people's windows, nor scribble on the walls of temples, shrines and public buildings. These are only a few samples of the injunctions that are imposed upon him.

II

The Government of Japan

In theory the Emperor of Japan is the source of all good and the fountain of all power. He owns every acre of the empire and occupies the throne by divine right. His authority is absolute, his judgment is infallible, and the people accept his edicts as the mandate of a god. But in practice, and by the voluntary act of the autocrat, there is quite as much liberality, democracy and self-government in Japan as there is in Germany.

The administration is divided into ten departments, each presided over by a minister of state. This cabinet is responsible only to the Emperor, by whom the ministers are appointed and dismissed at will. There is also a privy council whose function is to furnish advice either voluntarily or when it is asked for. There are three capital cities, Tokyo, Kyoto, and Osaka, and each, with a bit of adjacent country, is a federal district, administered by a governor whom the Emperor appoints. The rest of the empire is divided on the French system into prefectures or provinces, whose officers are elected by the people. The official organization is very much like that of France.

Judged by the American standard the Japanese are a much-governed people, the officials being numerous, their authority great, and all sorts of things which with us are left to private enterprise are there cared for or carried on by the central government.

The present constitution was proclaimed upon the 11th of February, 1889—the 2,549th anniversary of the foundation of the empire. It was an event worthy the commemoration of the civilized world, as, for the first time in history, an absolute monarch, who had inherited despotic power from twenty-five centuries of ancestors, voluntarily presented his subjects with the gift of self-government, a blessing for which billions of people in other parts of the world have fought and died. This act, as I have said, was without precedent. There was no compulsion, no fear; only a sublime sense of justice and a recognition of the rights of man. An autocrat, believed by his people to be of divine origin, stepped from his throne, and in the presence of his relatives of the Imperial family, the peers, nobles, the high functionaries of the empire, the chosen representatives of the people, and the members of the diplomatic corps, handed the Minister President of State rolls of parchment containing "The Constitu-

The Government of Japan

tion of the Empire of Japan," an Imperial decree creating a House of Peers and a House of Representatives, and a code of laws embracing 332 articles.

The constitution recognizes the sanctity of the Imperial title, and His Majesty remains, as before, the source of all power and law, but his functions are exercised only with the sanction of parliament. Only in the presence of an emergency, to protect the public safety, or avert a public calamity, can he suspend law, and it is expressly provided that all decrees issued in a recess of parliament must be approved by that body immediately after it next assembles. The Emperor has supreme command of the army and navy, determines their organization, has the power to make war, peace and treaties, to confer titles of nobility and other marks of honor, and to extend amnesties or pardons to persons convicted of crime.

On the other hand, political and civil liberty and a measure of self-government is recognized as the rights of the subject. He can change his abode at will. He cannot be arrested, detained, tried or punished except according to the methods set down in the laws of the empire. His house is his castle, and his right of property is sacred. His letters and papers are inviolable, and cannot be searched without his consent. He is entitled to the freedom of religion, speech and

The Yankees of the East

association, provided he does not exercise that right in a manner prejudicial to the public peace and welfare or interfere with the rights of others. The laws of the empire are enacted by parliament, subject to the approval of the Emperor, while on the other hand he can exercise no power except that granted him in the constitution, without the approval of parliament.

The parliament meets annually and consists of two branches, the House of Peers and the House of Representatives. The House of Peers is partly elected, partly hereditary, and partly appointed by the Emperor. It is composed of five classes of members, and when complete numbers 272, exclusive of the princes of the Imperial family, who are entitled to seats when they reach their majority. Princes not of the blood, and marquises who have reached the age of twenty-five are members by inheritance. The Counts, Viscounts, and Barons of the empire are allowed to elect one-fifth of their number to represent them. These elections recur with every parliament. Each city of certain population and each province is entitled to one member who does not belong to the nobility, and may be elected from among the fifteen male inhabitants who pay the highest amount of taxes on land, industry and trade. These sit for seven years, and are forty-three in number. Thirteen

The Government of Japan

are merchants, thirteen are large land-owners, four are railroad men, two are bankers, one is a miner, one a steamboat owner, and the remainder are capitalists. In addition to these the Emperor has the right to appoint ninety members of the House of Peers as a reward for scholarship or meritorious service to the state. His appointments are for life and are considered the highest honors the sovereign can bestow, except patents of nobility.

The House of Representatives consists of three hundred members elected every four years by ballot, under a system of limited suffrage. No man is entitled to vote unless he pays a minimum of fifteen yen ($7.50) annually as taxes. Of the present house 156 are farmers, forty-one merchants, twenty-one lawyers, fourteen journalists, nine bankers and one is a physician. The remainder have no business and are chiefly professional politicians.

There is now a majority in the parliament against the government, but the opposition is so divided into factions that it is difficult for them to unite upon any distinct line of policy. The House of Peers can be depended upon at any time and on any measure to sustain the administration, whatever it may be, but the adverse vote of the Chamber of Deputies or the passage of a resolution of lack of confidence is some-

The Yankees of the East

times although not necessarily followed by a change in the ministry, as in England and France.

Political parties are numerous in Japan. Twelve are recognized by the editor of the Blue Book in assigning members of parliament their political status. The Radical party numbers 105. Then come in order the Progressionists, the Constitutional Reform party, the National Union party, the Practical Business party, the Finance Reform party, the Party of Great Questions, the Patriotic party, the Party of Self-Government, the Society of Fellow Thinkers, and the Middle Province party.

The revenue of the government is derived from five sources: customs dues, land tax, income and license tax, tax on liquors, and receipts from telegraph and post offices, railways and other public works. The tax on land furnishes at least two-thirds of the entire revenue, and the tax on spirits about one-fifth. The income tax is the next largest source of revenue. The land tax is one-fifth of one per cent. upon the value of the land, which is generally appraised at its market value, both in the cities and the rural districts. The income tax is graduated. On all incomes between 300 and 1,000 yen the tax is $\frac{10}{100}$ of one per cent.; on incomes between 1,000 and 10,000 yen it is $\frac{15}{100}$ of one per cent.; between 10,000 and 20,000 yen it is $\frac{25}{100}$ of one

The Government of Japan

per cent., and above 30,000 a year it is $\frac{60}{100}$ of one per cent. There is also a tax of seven-tenths of one per cent. upon the issue of national and other banks. Stamps are required on all deeds, bonds and checks, receipts, bills and other legal and commercial papers. Every suit that is filed in court, either criminal or civil, is required to pay a tax in the form of adhesive stamps which are placed upon the papers. In criminal cases it is assessed with other costs upon the defendant.

There is a tax upon all forms of speculations, on all trades on the stock exchange, the rice exchange, the produce exchange and other open boards of trade. The tax on the sale and purchase of government bonds is quite high, amounting to six-tenths of one per cent. There is a heavy tax on saké, beer and other liquors, tobacco, patent medicines, and confectionery, and a less one on soyu (the popular national sauce) and yeast. All owners of vessels, junks, steamers, sailing vessels, row boats, sampans, and every other thing that floats, have to take out a license, and owners of land vehicles of every kind have to do the same. A tax is imposed upon all animals, horses, dogs, cows and cats. A sportsman has to pay for the privilege of owning a gun, one yen or fifty cents of our money each year, whether he uses it or not. The receipts from this source in 1894 were nearly

The Yankees of the East

thirty thousand dollars. There is a tax on watches and clocks, but it is merely nominal, and every person engaged in business, whether he sells newspapers on the street or owns a coal mine, or a cotton mill, even the geisha girls, the porters who handle your baggage at the railway station and the old women who sell rice cakes, chestnuts and confectionery at the corners of the streets have to pay a fee and secure a license. There is a tax of one-tenth of one per cent upon the net earnings of corporations, which increases gradually as the amount grows larger until it reaches a maximum of one-half of one per cent. It is difficult to find anybody in the empire of Japan, except the favored foreigners who are protected by treaties, that does not contribute something to the public treasury. But the taxation is so evenly distributed that no one feels the burden, or complains. There is no country in the world where taxes are paid so promptly and willingly. There is some grumbling because foreigners are exempt and the government is not allowed to impose more than five per cent duty upon imported goods, but both the government and the people are waiting patiently for the new treaties which recognize Japan as a civilized nation and allow her to regulate her own commerce.

Political campaigns in Japan are carried on very much as they are in this country. A prop-

The Government of Japan

erty qualification being necessary for suffrage, the volume of ballots cast is comparatively small; but the inability to exercise the right of suffrage does not interfere with the excitement of the peasants when election day comes round. The rich man does the voting; the poor man does the shouting. In order to vote in Japan a man must pay at least fifteen yen annually as taxes and show his receipts at the polling places. They have no ballots like ours, but a register which makes the elections absolutely accurate, and forbids any doubt of the result. When a voter comes to the polls, he is handed a long sheet of paper upon which he writes his own name, his residence, his occupation, the number of his tax receipt, and other statistical information, with the names of the candidates he prefers, so that his vote stands in his own handwriting and cannot be questioned. When the result of the election is declared these certificates are filed away in the county clerk's office, and are accessible to anyone.

On the English principle, a man can run for any office in any district. A citizen of Tokyo may represent in parliament the people who live at the extreme end of the empire if they elect him. Nor is it necessary for a man to have the property qualification required for suffrage in order to be a candidate for office. He may be as poor as Job's turkey, and may never have had

The Yankees of the East

the right to vote, but he can run for parliament just the same, and if elected is allowed to take his seat.

There is a strict law regulating campaigns and political associations. No public meeting can be held without a license from the police, and no club or association of more than six members can be organized for any purpose without filing at police headquarters a list of officers and members, with their residence, a copy of the constitution and by-laws, or some memorandum setting forth the object of the organization. No person other than a qualified voter can apply to the police for a license to hold a political meeting. Soldiers, sailors of the navy, members of the national militia, government employés, instructors and students in public schools, minors and women are absolutely prohibited from participating in public meetings. No foreigner can speak at a political meeting. No political meeting can be held in the open air. No political speech can be made, nor any political proposition offered or discussed at patriotic festivals, religious celebrations, social gatherings, or at any other assembly without formal notice to and permission from the police. No person is allowed to carry arms at a political meeting. No political association can carry any flag, ensign, standard or banner except the national flag of Japan. Should any political association be

The Government of Japan

deemed injurious to peace and order, the minister of home affairs may suspend or suppress it; and any political meeting may be prohibited or dissolved at the discretion of the police when in their judgment it is injurious to peace and order.

But limited suffrage has its drawbacks. In the summer of 1895, while I was in Japan, there was an election for members of the Tokyo city assembly. In the Hongo ward there were but three qualified voters besides the rival candidates, Messrs. Seki and Kazama. Each of these gentlemen were confident of one vote, and the result depended upon the ballot of the Marquis Asono, who happened to be absent from the city. Both candidates made every possible effort to induce him to return to the city in time to cast his ballot, but he was detained away, and the election, being a tie, was declared null and void. The candidates each received two solitary votes, one of which they cast for themselves. A new election was to be called as soon as the Marquis Asono returned to the city and was willing to exercise his constitutional privilege.

It is very rare to find a Japanese woman in politics. The only notable case that I have heard of is that of Madam Hatoyama, who is one of the most remarkable women in Japan. Her husband, Dr. Hatoyama, is among the leaders of the progressionist party, and the principal of an academy or select school for teaching the high branches, patronized by Count Okuma, the progressionist leader. Madam Hatoyama was one of the first women of Japan to receive a foreign education, and upon her return to the country she took an ambitious, independent position which attracted a great deal of criticism and unfavorable comment. Among those who defended her was Dr. Hatoyama, a young man of profound learning and advanced views. This little incident soon made them acquainted and ended in their marriage. Some years after, when Dr. Hatoyama entered his campaign as a candidate of the progressionist party for parliament, his wife took the stump in his interest and made speeches everywhere in his district. She also called personally upon voters, and solicited their support. She is at present a teacher in the academy of which her husband is principal, and takes an active part in all progressionist movements.

Free speech is permitted under police regulation, if that is not a contradiction of terms, and seven members of the chamber of deputies were fined 20 yen ($10) each last summer for forming a political club and holding a political meeting without giving notice to the authorities as required by article 21 of the law governing public assemblies and political associations. Curiously enough, Mr Suyehiro, one of the defendants, introduced in parliament the very law

The Government of Japan

under which he was punished. It requires all organizations or associations of more than six members to file with the registrar at the city hall their names and objects and copies of their constitutions and by-laws, if they have any. This law was intended to prohibit secret societies. There are masonic lodges in nearly all of the principal cities, and a few natives belong to them, but they hold their meetings in the foreign concessions which are under consular jurisdiction exclusively and exempt from Japanese control.

When the new treaty goes into effect in 1899 consular jurisdiction is abolished and all foreigners will be subject to the laws of the empire just the same as the natives. While the treaty was under discussion in the United States Senate the question was raised as to whether the law of Japan which prohibits secret societies would apply to the masonic and other orders, and an assurance was given by the Japanese government that it would not. This point was discussed at length between Secretary Gresham and the Japanese minister at Washington and the former was assured that it would be interpreted to exempt benevolent and charitable associations. Officials of the Japanese foreign department inform me that while there is no expressed exemption an assurance has been given in the correspondence with the powers concerning the new treaties that will be recognized. They also say that there are many societies for social and benevolent purposes that are not registered at police headquarters; that the law is strictly applied to political organizations only, and although it can be construed to cover every form of association it is equally easy to interpret it so as to exempt those that are intended for innocent purposes.

The case referred to is the first conspicuous violation of the law governing public meetings and political associations. It appears that the defendants, who are active members of political parties opposed to the government, formed a coalition for mutual support and consultation, with the hope of being able to consolidate the opposition to the ministry before the next meeting of parliament. They held several conferences at a popular restaurant, which they claim were merely informal gatherings of men of the same views, and then called a public meeting in one of the largest halls in the city without securing the permission of the police authorities as required. There was no attempt at secrecy in either case. The meeting was announced in the newspapers several days in advance, and was attended by both the police and the reporters. The hall was packed with people and twenty persons were invited to make addresses. Fourteen of the speakers were stopped

MARQUIS ITO, PRIME MINISTER.

The Government of Japan

in the midst of their remarks by the police and politely invited "to reserve the remainder of their discourses," as the newspapers said. The excuse for these interruptions was the use of intemperate language concerning the policy of the government. But there seems to have been an intentional and deliberate defiance of the law on the part of the politicians, and, on the other hand, the government took that occasion to make an example of those members of parliament for the benefit of others who were trying to stir up an insurrection in Japan.

Under ordinary circumstances the government is very liberal toward the press and public gatherings, but occasionally brings down an iron hand in a manner that would do credit to the czar, and its policy after the treaty of peace with China is evidence that Marquis Ito, the prime minister, and his associates realized that Japan was then passing through the most critical period in its recent history. Not only have the opposition newspapers been suppressed to an extent that was never known before, but several political associations have been disbanded by orders of the police, which appear in the following form:

"It is hereby announced that the Minister of State for Home Affairs, deeming the organization called the Seiyu Yushi-kai injurious to good order and the public peace, forbids the further meetings and continuance of said association, in accordance with article 29 of the law of public meetings and political associations of the 26th year of Meiji.

SONODA YASUKATA,
"Inspector-General Metropolitan Police."

Copies of such notices are served upon the president and other officials of interdicted organizations and are published in the official gazette.

But, considering the rapid and radical revolution that has taken place in Japanese affairs, it is very remarkable that the peace of the empire has been preserved as it has, and that the liberality of the government has endured a test that would not have been successful in many other countries. The reformation of 1868 was undoubtedly the most remarkable that has ever occurred in human history. Revolutions are usually the result of circumstances and irritation within the nation itself, even when the direct cause may have been found elsewhere. But in Japan the destruction of the old despotism and the introduction of modern standards of religious and civil liberty was directly due to foreign influence, and the result must amaze even those who were instrumental in bringing it about. There have been political eruptions and upheavals in Japan because of a lack of harmony and the existence of jealousy among leaders, but the ease and order with which a semi-civilized peo-

The Government of Japan

ple have transformed themselves into a state of civilization that will compare well with that of the nations of Europe and America, and surpasses several of them, has no parallel.

The great difficulty in Japan at present, as in all new governments, is the ambition of certain men, who consider themselves wiser than others, to try their hand in the administration of affairs; but the criticism of those who are in by those who are out is no more severe than in the United States, Germany or Great Britain, and party feeling is by no means as bitter as it is in France, where may be found conditions more nearly similar than anywhere else.

The peace of Japan and the perpetuation of the government, of which Marquis Ito is the foremost spirit, has been largely due, however, to the petty divisions into which the opposition has been broken. If there were only two parties in Japan, as in England and the United States, there would have been frequent changes in the administration; but, as in France, there are a dozen political organizations, each advocating a different policy and criticising the persons in power from a different standpoint.

There are also men of genius who belong to none of them, but have their own ideas of good government, and ride their hobbies with a zeal equal to that displayed by Senator Stewart in support of free coinage. The most of them are sincere, but all are inexperienced and are suffering from mental and political indigestion. Each has his followers for personal or political reasons of sufficient number to keep him in parliament or sustain a newspaper in which he is able to express his views. There is no thought of treason to the emperor, nor to the men who are executing what is supposed to be his policy, but everyone is zealous and patriotic, and confident that his particular plan is necessary to bring this Asiatic state up to the same standard of civilization that is found in Europe and North America. They have read of foreign institutions without being able to realize clearly what they are, and thousands of theories and innumerable laws are the results of hot-house education and inexperience.

It must be remembered that the men who are at present in office swept away the whole ancient organization of an empire, which had existed for more than 2,500 years, and was the outgrowth of the life and labors, the thoughts and feelings, the needs and the aspirations of several hundred generations of men. This was replaced by an imported civilization, which was imported from foreign countries like any other commodity. Education, military and naval systems, a judicial organization, financial methods, a foreign policy and all other features of the government were brought in with foreign garments, the tele-

The Government of Japan

graph, the telephone, the electric light and the perfecting printing press, and introduced among the people by a forced process. With a vast range of policies and practices to select from, the men of genius who directed the rapid evolution of Japan naturally found perplexing problems, and it is a wonder that the thinkers and statesmen of that empire did not find greater difficulty in selecting and retaining what is good and suitable and rejecting what is bad and unsuitable to their people.

And the readiness and facility with which the people accepted the new manner of things is even more remarkable. It is true that they had been trained to submission for centuries, and that the highest virtue in their moral calendar was respect for the imperial power. Otherwise it might not have been so easy to revolutionize the social system of 40,000,000 people in a few years. This respect for and submission to the recognized authority is the safeguard of Japan to-day, but with the education of the people it may sometime appear that the supposed divinity of the Mikado is a mistake, and the toleration of the soshi class, consisting of patriotic but inexperienced youths, who are educated in a way that is of no practical good to themselves and most pernicious to the peace of the state, may result in the development of a socialistic party that will be more dangerous than any opposition the present government has yet encountered.

While there has been a considerable amount of legislation that is crude and contradictory, the courts of Japan are as pure and just as any in the world. The confusion that arises from the lack of a proper code, and an attempt to apply laws which contradict each other, makes it necessary for the judiciary to exercise a great deal of common sense, which, after all, is the best rule for testing the rights and wrongs of men. There are no long delays in judicial proceedings; there are no devious and concealed paths by which a criminal may escape punishment through the aid of a shrewd and skillful lawyer. Justice is swift and sure. A man who commits a murder on Monday is usually sentenced to the gallows or to life imprisonment on the northern island before the end of the week, and he is either buried or on his way northward before the expiration of a fortnight.

The object of the courts seems to be to ascertain the facts, and not the law in the case, and when an offender is proved guilty no technicalities are allowed to interfere.

At the state penitentiary, on the island of Ishikawa, just south of this city, we saw one day in a workshop, polishing the surface of a beautiful cloisonne vase, a man who, as judge of the district court less than a year before, sentenced to

The Government of Japan

the terms they are now serving many of the prisoners who work beside him. He accepted a bribe for the misapplication of his judicial power, and went to the island with a speed that offers a wholesome example for the purification of the bench to some other nations.

The peril, not only to foreigners but to the principal officials of the Japanese government, is from the "soshi," a class of agitators similar to the socialists of the United States and Europe, who are found in every large city and constitute the most reckless and dangerous portion of the community. It was a member of this class who attempted to assassinate Li Hung Chang, and they make it necessary for Marquis Ito, the prime minister, Count Mutsu, the minister of foreign affairs, and other conspicuous men to surround themselves with detectives and a military guard.

The soshi are mostly young men. Many of them are disappointed office-seekers. Others have been discharged from the public service for incompetency or other reasons, and prefer to make politics a profession and pick up a living as they can, instead of earning honest wages. After the restoration of the Mikado and the introduction of modern reforms into Japan, thousands of ambitious young men flocked to the capital and to other large cities hoping to better their condition. They got a smattering of education with the expectation of fitting themselves

The Yankees of the East

to hold office under the government and positions in commercial houses. Many of them were successful, but thousands failed, and being unable to obtain employment, and unwilling to return to their former homes in the farming villages of the interior, they consider society responsible for their misfortunes and live to revenge themselves upon society—prompted by desperation and despair. They are generally possessed of more than an ordinary degree of intelligence, and the free schools have given them the knowledge that "is a dangerous thing." Many of them have a gift of oratory, and have become political agitators, disagreeable, noisy demagogues who are constantly stirring up trouble and dissatisfaction among the coolie class by false information and fallacious arguments.

A common interest and the necessity of self-protection against the police has caused them to form themselves into secret societies, which have more or less rivalry among themselves, and have leaders who are always ready to throw their influence and the support of their followers in the interest of any one who is willing to pay their price. Therefore at election times these soshi are very active in the interest of the politicians who employ them. Just now they are exceedingly pestiferous.

Like all men of their kind, the average soshi is a coward, and more disagreeable than danger-

The Government of Japan

ous, but their societies attract all the cranks in the country — the Guiteaus and the August Spieses of Japan — who become excited under their oratory and are liable to do anything in the way of crime.

Since the restoration there have been six attempts at assassination in Japan, but fortunately four of them were unsuccessful, although in the other cases two of the most valuable lives in the empire were sacrificed by crazy fanatics in the name of patriotism.

In 1873 nine men attacked the carriage of Iwakura Tomomi, the Prime Minister, just as he was leaving the palace grounds after an interview with the Emperor. His coachman and footman were cut down, but he escaped the clutches of his assailants, leaped into the moat that encloses the walls of the castle, and escaped in the darkness with a few slight wounds. Those who attacked him were samurai, the class of soldiers in old Japan who corresponded to the knights of feudal days in Europe. When the ancient system of government was dissolved they were left without employment. Many went into the army, and it was proposed to pension those who were past the military age. Mr. Iwakura was suspected of opposing this plan, and for that reason they wanted to put him out of the way.

In 1878 Okubo Toshimichi, then Prime Minister, and unquestionably the ablest statesman of

The Yankees of the East

modern Japan, was assassinated upon the public highway by a half-insane fellow named Shimada, who was opposed to the introduction of modern ideas and believed that he could put a stop to progress by removing its chief apostle.

On the 11th of February, 1888, the very day that the constitution of Japan was proclaimed, Viscount Mori Arinori, Minister of Education, was murdered at the door of his residence by a religious fanatic named Nishino Buntaro, who sought to avenge a fancied profanation of a Shinto temple, which Viscount Mori was accused of entering without removing his shoes.

In October, 1889, when Count Okuma Shigenobu, then Minister of Foreign Affairs, was returning from a cabinet meeting at the Imperial palace, a soshi named Kurushima Tsuneki threw a dynamite bomb into his carriage. It exploded and shattered his right leg, which had to be amputated, but he recovered and is still one of the foremost men of the empire—the leader of the progressionist party. The motive in this case was a belief that the minister had surrendered too many of the rights of Japan in making commercial treaties with foreign powers.

In May, 1891, the Czarevitch of Russia—the present emperor—who was making a tour of the country, was attacked at the little town of Otsu by a soshi named Tsuda Sanzo because he represented a government that was supposed to be

The Government of Japan

hostile to Japan. The assassin was stricken down by the Duke of Athens, who was accompanying his cousin.

And finally in March, 1895, Li Hung Chang was shot by a soshi when he was on his way to a meeting of the Peace Envoys at Shimenoseki.

In each of these cases the assassins were prompted by mistaken patriotism, and with the exception of the first they belonged to the wretched and mischievous soshi class, who profess to be the guardians of liberty, but are really its worst enemies. They are possessed of distorted ideas and unbridled passions; and, as no honorable career is open to them, often seek notoriety by striking at some conspicuous mark, and creating a sensation.

Appointments in the civil service of Japan, including both the executive departments and the judiciary, are almost entirely made after examinations and are for life. The diplomatic and consular service is permanent, and those who enter it are required to submit to a special examination; but they cannot be appointed to an office in any other branch of the government without passing the regular examinations. The cabinet and the heads of bureaus change with the politics of the government, just as they do in other countries, on the theory that the higher grades of officials should be in sympathy with the policy of the administration; but as a matter

The Yankees of the East

of fact very few changes occur among the bureau officers. The judiciary is not changed except by impeachment.

In the civil service there are four classes: (1) The han-nin, which includes all of the clerks, stenographers and other employés of the several executive departments, except certain specified officials who will be mentioned hereafter; (2) the so-nin, who are the chiefs of divisions, heads of bureaus, directors of various institutions under the auspices of the government, and members of the consulate corps; (3) the choku-nin, who are members of the ministry and their vice-ministers, members of the diplomatic corps and officials about the imperial palace; (4) the yatoi, who include everything else not specified by law or engaged in the regular routine, such as interpreters, dispatch agents, translators employed for special purposes, confidential and secret-service men. Messengers, janitors, coolies and other menial attendants are termed yo-nin and are appointed by the heads of departments as needed. Their salaries are paid out of miscellaneous appropriations.

The han-nin class are appointed after competitive examinations, which any candidate may enter, whether he be a prince or a peasant. The examining boards are permanent, as with us, and endeavor to make the test as practical as possible, and to determine the comparative usefulness of

The Government of Japan

the candidates. At the close of the examination lists are certified to the secretary of the cabinet in the order of merit, and the appointments are made from these lists during the year following as vacancies occur. Exception is made in favor of graduates of the Imperial university upon whom degrees have been conferred, and no candidate is eligible for examination except those educated in the public schools and certain private schools recognized by the government.

A preliminary examination for the so-nin class is held at Tokyo each year. Applicants are first required to write a thesis, and are then examined upon it. If they pass this ordeal they are examined upon: 1. The Constitution; 2. The Criminal Law; 3. The Civil Law; 4. Administrative Law; 5. Political Economy; 6. International Law. Then there are four other topics upon either of which the candidate may elect to be examined: Finance; Commercial Law; Law of Criminal Procedure, and Law of Civil Procedure.

It is supposed that the man who stands at the head of the list is appointed to the first vacancy, and that is the general practice, although exceptions do occur occasionally in favor of some young man with strong personal influence or a political pull, but a good reason is invariably given for his selection, and no exception is made of persons who have not passed the examination.

The Yankees of the East

The consistency of the government in this respect has a conspicuous illustration in the person of the son of one of the most influential members of the cabinet. He has an excellent English education, has spent the greater part of his life abroad and is a graduate of Cambridge university, England; but he is deficient in his native language, and has twice failed to pass examinations in that particular. He occupies the position of interpreter in his father's department, which comes under the yatoi class, and in the meantime is studying Japanese for the purpose of taking another examination.

Appointments are always made to the lowest grade of the han-nin class, where the salary is only 12 yen, or $6.00, a month. This applies alike to doctors of law and doctors of philosophy who may have taken degrees at the university and to the boy from the high school who passes the examination. Promotions are made as vacancies occur, by examination and record for efficiency. The highest salary paid in the han-nin class is 120 yen, or $60 a month.

Examinations for the han-nin class are held in the several departments as vacancies occur. Each department has its own board, presided over by one of its chief officials. The examinations are much like those for the so-nin class, but especial attention is given to the qualifica-

The Government of Japan

tions of candidates for the duties they are expected to perform.

The so-nin class is filled by competitive examinations. There are several grades of officials under this classification, receiving salaries from 125 yen to 200 yen a month. The consular corps is usually filled from the members of the so-nin class, and promotions are made on the record of the officials. Their commissions are signed by the prime minister and bear the cabinet seal.

The choku-nin are supposed to be appointed by the emperor, but as a matter of fact the prime minister acts for him in this, as he does in nearly every other executive capacity. The emperor selects the prime minister whenever a change of administration is demanded by the parliament or he may himself consider it expedient, and the prime minister selects his cabinet just as is done in England and France, or by the president of the United States, subject to the approval of the sovereign. The ministers are naturally allowed to choose their immediate assistants, as with us, but nominally the latter receive their authority from the emperor. The same is true of the members of the diplomatic corps, who are selected by the minister of foreign affairs after consultation with the prime minister. The choku-nin are not required to pass an examination. Their commissions bear the imperial seal.

The Yankees of the East

The minister of the household, who has charge of the person of his majesty and all affairs at the palace, is, of course, selected by the emperor himself, and is not often changed. His position and relations are not affected by politics. He is like the grand chamberlain at the European courts and occupies a close personal relation with the Mikado. The emperor is supposed also to select the various officials that are employed in the household department, and they are seldom changed, for obvious reasons, unless he promotes them to positions of greater dignity and emolument.

The prime minister receives a salary of 9,600 yen per year. The compensation of a cabinet minister is 6,000 yen, $3,000, a year in gold, but they are furnished with residences and servants, an allowance for purposes of entertainment, and, in fact, all of their household expenses except clothing and food. The government owns a large number of fine mansions. Some of them were confiscated with the other property of the daimyos at the time of the revolution, but more have been erected on modern architectural designs within the last twenty-five years. They are usually filled with European furniture, although in most of them some rooms are arranged on the Japanese plan, especially those for the accommodation of the servants. Each of

The Government of Japan

these houses has a major domo, or steward, and a staff of servants who are permanent, like the furniture, bedding, china and the ornaments that decorate the walls.

These residences are assigned to the several members of the cabinet, the presiding officers of the two houses of parliament and other high officials, and when changes are made in the administration the old occupant moves out and his successor moves in. There is no disturbance in the kitchen or in the stable. The new tenant can make changes in the arrangement of the place if he likes, and can discharge the servants if they are not satisfactory. He is master of the premises as long as he lives there, just as the president of the United States is at the White house, but when his term of office expires he must move.

The vice-ministers, or assistants to the members of the cabinet, are not furnished residences and are paid only 4,000 yen, or $2,000, a year, but that is considered a handsome salary in Japan, such as the presidents of banks and the managers of large business enterprises receive. It would be considered fair compensation for the general manager of a railroad, or the president of an insurance company, although in private life they have a way of making presents to faithful officials at the end of each year in ad-

The Yankees of the East

dition to their salaries. The heads of bureaus receive corresponding amounts, generally $1,500 and $1,800 a year.

The members of the Japanese ministry do not look after the details of their departments so closely as heads of our executive departments at Washington, but leave that for the vice-ministers. They attend meetings of the cabinet two or three times a week, consult together over matters of politics, and give general directions as to affairs. The vice-ministers remain in the background and attend to business. They reach their offices at an early hour and leave them at a late hour every day, receiving visitors, conducting the correspondence and attending to the routine, which they are allowed to do as long as they adhere to the line of policy that their chief marks out for them. Sometimes they do not see him for days, but they usually prepare a budget of official business, which they tuck into a portfolio and send to him at his residence on cabinet days for him to lay before the council of ministers. The vice-ministers are bright, progressive young men of executive talent and brilliant attainments. Four of those at present in office were educated in the United States. Two are graduates of Harvard and one of Yale, while the other took a law course in New York city.

When you call upon the minister or vice-

A JAPANESE RESIDENCE.

The Government of Japan

minister of a Japanese department you are shown into a reception-room that is furnished with ugly Brussels carpets and American furniture. There is usually a table in the center surrounded with uncomfortable chairs and a set of Japanese smoking apparatus placed upon it for the accommodation of visitors. The windows are decorated with white shades, lace curtains and heavy brocade hangings, the latter being the only article of Japanese manufacture visible. The walls are covered with imported paper-hangings, maps of Japan, China, Europe and America, and usually a big Connecticut clock. In the corners are black walnut "what-nots," with a few books—official reports and that sort of thing—and one day I saw a janitor dusting them with a pair of bellows, which I thought was a pretty good idea. He blew the dust down on the shelf behind the books, where it can accumulate until it amounts to enough to cart away. A few of the clerks are barefooted and some of them sit on the floor to do their work, but in most of the departments they dress in foreign garments, and use desks and tables of foreign design and often foreign manufacture.

The government buildings are nearly all of French and German architecture, being designed by imported architects or young men who were sent to Paris, Vienna and Berlin to study architecture years ago. Most of them are built of

The Yankees of the East

brick, which isn't suitable for an earthquake country like Japan, and they are usually out of repair.

In addition to the cabinet of ministers the emperor has a privy council whose function it is to tender him advice. It may be larger or smaller, according to his wishes, but now is composed of twelve men—ex-members of the ministry, who have retired from active life, princes from the imperial family, uncles of his majesty—members of the nobility, and others who are distinguished for learning and wisdom. They have no authority, but are a sort of honorary fifth wheel to the government, receiving salaries of 4,000 yen per year. They are expected to do a lot of heavy thinking and act as a safeguard to protect the emperor from the mistakes of his ministers. They have no regular dates of meeting, but assemble whenever the emperor sends for them, and he sometimes presides over their deliberations. During the recent war they were called together quite frequently, and the emperor usually submits all matters of national policy to them before giving his own sanction. While he has great confidence in Marquis Ito, the present prime minister, who is the ablest man in Japan, the emperor very frequently exercises his own discretion in matters of state, and has repeatedly declined to approve propositions and appointments which were supported by the entire cabinet.

III
The Imperial Family

The Emperor of Japan is supposed to be descended from the gods. I believe he is the only man on earth who claims divine parentage. In geology Japan is the youngest of lands, and of recent volcanic origin. The authentic history of the country begins with the eighth century. The people had almanacs and means of measuring time as far back as the sixth century. The traditions are pretty well defined from about the beginning of the Christian era. The oldest documents in the archives of the government were written in 712, and the antiquity of the imperial family is unparalleled among nations. The line runs back, unbroken, as far as that of the popes of Rome with absolute certainty, and Mutsu Hito not only claims to be the 122d emperor of the same family but to have received his crown by unbroken succession from Jimmu Tenno, who ascended the throne in the year 660 B. C.

The official history of the empire of Japan says that "from the time that Amaterasu-Omikami made Ninigi-no-Mikoto descend from the heavens and subject to his administrative sway

The Yankees of the East

Okuninusi-no-Mikoto and other offspring of the deities, descendants of divine beings have sat upon the throne generation after generation. Each sovereign, faithful to the spirit of his divine ancestors and to the administrative policy bequeathed by their divine descendants, transmitted the reins of power to his successor, thus preserving the continuity of the imperial dynasty and achieving the aim of good government. Descended in a direct line from the heavenly deities, the emperor has stood unshaken in his high place through all generations, his prestige and dignity immutable from time immemorial, and independent of all the vicissitudes of the world about him."

The period before the reign of the Emperor Jimmu, seven centuries before Christ, when the Japanese assume that their actual history begins is called Jindai—the age of the deities. Two gods of minor rank were commanded by the supreme sovereign of heaven to form a country out of certain islands that were floating in space, and in obedience to such instructions Japan became a nation. The divine pair then were made husband and wife and gave birth to the ancestors of Mutsu Hito.

In the Shiba park, near Tokyo, there is a shrine dedicated to the memory of these divinities. It is said to have been erected in the year 1005, and it is one of the most beautiful exam-

The Imperial Family

ples of ancient Japanese architecture. Within the shrine is kept a mirror, a crystal and a sword —the emblems of imperial power—which were handed down from the divine authors of the nation to Jimmu, and by him transmitted to the present occupant of the throne. The emperor goes to this shrine to worship between September 16 and 21, which is the period assigned to the creation of Japan.

The mirror is the emblem of conscience. When the emperor looks into it he sees the ruler of forty-one millions of people, and is reminded of his responsibilities. The crystal is the emblem of purity. When he looks upon it he is reminded of what his life and his government should be. The sword is the emblem of power. When he looks upon it he is reminded of the authority and dignity of his office, which should be used always and only to maintain the right, and correct the wrong. A member of the imperial family is the custodian of these relics, and arranges the programme for the September ceremonies.

While the present emperor is not unmindful of his divine origin, he has shown himself to be more of a human personality than any of his predecessors. Until the reformation in 1868 he and those who had previously occupied the throne were practically the prisoners of the tycoon, or shogun, as he was more often called—the

The Yankees of the East

generalissimo of the army—and were seldom allowed to leave the shelter of the yellow walls that surround the grounds of the imperial palace at Kyoto. He knew nothing of his subjects and was unknown to them. He was too sacred for the eyes of ordinary mortals to look upon, and even now when his name is mentioned all of the old-fashioned Japanese make a low bow.

The respect of the press of Japan for the Mikado is expressed by printing his name in capitals. For example, one paper says:

"The nation will echo the words of its EMPEROR, who says: 'WE were constrained to take up arms against China for no other reason than OUR desire to secure for the Orient an enduring peace."

After death the emperors became deities and were enshrined with the other gods.

Since 1868, however, the emperor has gradually taken the reins of power more and more into his own hands until he is now quite as much the ruler of his country as King Humbert is of Italy or Francis Joseph of Austria. He does not show as much nervous activity as Emperor William, but he has more to do with the administration of affairs than Queen Victoria or the regent of Spain. He presides quite often at the meetings of the cabinet and usually attends the sessions of the council. While he is sensible enough to keep his hands off the executive branches of the government, and permits his ministers to

The Imperial Family

look after details, he requires them to consult him concerning all matters of public policy and to report promptly all events of importance. For example, every important order that was issued from the navy or war departments during the late war was submitted to him before it was promulgated, and a copy of every report from the army in China and Korea was furnished him as soon as received.

He takes a great interest in industrial and commercial affairs, and has often added from his privy purse to the subsidies voted by parliament for the encouragement of new enterprises. He examines closely into the revenues and expenditures of the government.

The emperor was only 16 years of age when in February, 1868, he received the envoys of foreign nations at the palace of Kyoto with uncovered face. Before that time no foreigner had ever looked upon a Mikado and the eyes of his own subjects had seldom seen his divine person. He concealed himself even from the nobles of the court and at his receptions the throne was protected by curtains.

The ancient throne of Japan is now on exhibition in the imperial museum in Tokyo—the one that was used until about twenty years ago. It consists of a platform eighteen inches high and about twelve feet square. The floor is covered with the thick matting that you find in every

The Yankees of the East

house, and was spread with rugs of exquisite embroidery, while in the center was a silken cushion, upon which his imperial majesty squatted like a tailor or a Turk. Handsomely carved and lacquered posts supported a square canopy made of white silk, delicately embroidered with the Mikado's crest. This canopy concealed him from all eyes except those of his personal attendants, through whom he communicated with the public and who draped him in his imperial robes. Some of those robes are now exhibited in the same room with the throne, along with a lot of swords and saddles and other military equipments that were worn by the shoguns, and cases of earthen images of men and horses that were used for interment in the graves of illustrious personages after the custom of burying the chief retainers alive with their lords was abandoned.

There also can be seen the ancient imperial carriage which was drawn by a bullock, the palanquins in which the Mikado and the shogun and the members of the imperial family used to ride about, and a model of the state barge, which was known as the "ship of heaven and earth," and was propelled by sixty-four oars, like the galleys of Antony and Cleopatra.

In an adjoining room are several cases containing relics of Christianity that were left in Japan when the Franciscan and Jesuit mission-

The Imperial Family

aries were driven out of the country nearly 300 years ago. St. Francis Xavier spent most of his life in Japan, and might have evangelized the country, for noblemen, Buddhist priests, men of learning and military commanders embraced the faith with the same alacrity as the poor and ignorant, and by the year 1582 the number of Japanese professing the Christian faith was estimated at 1,000,000 souls. And so favorable were both the princes and the people that they sent an embassy to the pope to beseech his favor and acknowledge his supremacy. But in 1596 an edict was issued by a jealous shogun, who thought the people ought to obey him instead of God, expelling every missionary and commanding every convert to renounce the faith.

Many of the presents that were brought from the Vatican are preserved and exhibited in the museum, with holy pictures, rosaries, crucifixes and other emblems of religion that were concealed by the faithful during the persecution; and there are several curious fumi-ita or "trampling boards" — oblong blocks of metal with figures of Christ and the crucifixion, the descent from the cross, the Madonna and Child, and other representations of the most sacred character, upon which persons suspected of the crime of Christianity were obliged to trample in order to testify to their abjuration of the "depraved faith."

The Yankees of the East

But the emperor wears no embroidered robes to-day, and his throne is simply a gilded chair, from which he can see the members of his court; and no screen of silk conceals him from them. While he is not as accessible as some of the European sovereigns, and never appears in public except upon some important function of state, he has become a familiar figure to the upper classes and the members of the diplomatic corps, who are invited to the palace several times a year and are asked to accompany him at military reviews, the inauguration of public enterprises and on other occasions when his majesty participates.

The palace grounds include twenty-six acres, to which strangers are never admitted except upon the invitation of the sovereign or by a permit from the minister of the household, which is exceedingly difficult to obtain. There are riding courts, rifle ranges, gymnasiums, groves, gardens, fish-ponds and other facilities for exercise and amusement, but his majesty seldom utilizes them, for he is not fond of sport, and is afflicted with rheumatism to an extent that often seriously interferes with his movements. He has several palaces in different parts of the country which he never visits, and magnificent game preserves where he never shoots. There is an imperial yacht in the navy, also, but he never goes to sea.

THE PRINCE IMPERIAL.

The Imperial Family

He is of a serious temperament, lacks social qualities and is so occupied with ceremonies and receptions that he has very little time to himself. From all I can hear he works as hard as President Cleveland and has an equally solemn sense of his responsibilities. Some years ago he attempted to learn English and German, but gave them up as a heavy task. On public occasions he wears a heavily frogged and gilded uniform as generalissimo of the army, with a sword of modern pattern in a golden scabbard and a hilt loaded with diamonds and other jewels.

The prince imperial is almost continually ill, and is the object of great anxiety. He is under the care of a commission of three or four of the foremost physicians of Japan, but they are very discreet in discussing the condition of their patient, and people can only judge when he is better or worse by their looks and actions. His trouble is water on the brain. His head is abnormally large, and although his intellect is bright and he is in full possession of his mental powers he is peculiarly sensitive to diseases of the brain and nervous system. In fact, he has not only been under treatment ever since his birth, but the first prince imperial died of the same disease, which seems to be hereditary. All of the imperial children are troubled in the same manner.

The emperor has had twelve children. Two

died on the day of their birth, one lived nine months, one thirteen months, one fourteen months, two eighteen months and one two years. He has four children living, three girls, born in 1888, 1890 and 1891, and one boy. The Countess Sono was the mother of four, the Countess Chigusa and the Countess Yanagawara of three each, Mme. Hashunato and Mme. Hamuro of one each. All the sons but one in the the family were born of the Countess Yanagiwara, mother of the prince imperial. She is a daughter of Count Yanagiwara, who lives in Tokyo and is very highly respected. The countess, who became a concubine in 1875, is said to be a very able woman, although she has little beauty.

The following is the list as it appears in the official directory of the empire:

CHILDREN.

A prince was born to the Emperor the 18th day of the 9th month of the 6th year of Meiji (1873) and died on the same day.

A princess was born to the Emperor by Princess Hashimoto Natsuko the 13th day of the 11th month of the 6th year of Meiji (1873) and died on the same day.

SHIGEKO, Ume no Miya, daughter of the Emperor, born the 25th day of the 1st month, 8th year of Meiji (Jan. 25, 1875). (Died June 8, 1876.)

YUKIHITO, Take no Miya, the second son of the Emperor by Princess Yanagiwara, born the 23d day of September, 1877. (Died July 27, 1878.)

YOSHIHITO, Haru no Miya, the third son of the Emperor, born the 31st day of August, 1879. He was

The Imperial Family

nominated heir-apparent on August 31, 1887. Proclaimed the Crown Prince (Kōtaishi) the 3rd of November, 1889, and decorated with the Grand Order of Merit and Grand Insignia of the Imperial Chrysanthemum, appointed an Ensign in the Imperial bodyguard infantry on the same day.

AKIKO, Shige no Miya, daughter of the Emperor, born the 3rd day of August, 1881. (Died September 7, 1883.)

FUMIKO, Masu no Miya, daughter of the Emperor, born the 26th day of January, 1883. (Died September 8, 1883.)

SHIGEKO, Hisa no Miya, daughter of the Emperor, born the 10th day of February, 1886. (Died April 4, 1887.)

MICHIHITO, Aki no Miya, the fourth son of the Emperor, by Princess Sono, born the 22nd day, of August, 1887. (Died November 12, 1888.)

MASAKO, Tsune no Miya, daaughter of the Emperor by Princess Sono, born the 30th day of September, 1888.

FUSAKO, Kane no Miya, seventh daughter of the Emperor, born the 29th of January, 1890.

NOBUKO, Fumi no Miya, eighth daughter of the Emperor, born the 8th of August, 1891.

Yuki Hito, the first heir-apparent, was born in 1877, and lived less than a year. Yoshi Hito, the present prince imperial, was born in 1879, and was proclaimed heir to the throne in 1887. Under the constitution of Japan the emperor may select his own successor, who must be of royal blood in order to continue the present line of succession, which is traced back 2,500 years, but the candidate need not necessarily be the

The Yankees of the East

emperor's own son, nor the son of the empress. In 1892, when the prince imperial was thirteen years old he was made a lieutenant in the imperial bodyguard, and now at sixteen is colonel of a fancy regiment.

The prince imperial has been brought up in a very democratic manner. For several years he attended the school that is kept exclusively for the sons of princes and nobles, and his treatment and instruction were no different from those of any other boy in the institution. He had to be as punctual in the morning and attend to his lessons as studiously during the school hours, and no exceptions were made in his favor; but a year or so ago it was thought that the course of study was a little too severe for his weak brain, and he has since been under the care of a "grand master," or tutor, Gen. Oku, who has charge of his education, assisted by a Mr. Adachi and several other teachers. He is being taught English, French and German, arithmetic, geography, history, the natural sciences and military tactics. The emperor takes a great interest in his education, and the empress even more, although he is not her son, and they are both exceedingly anxious that he shall have what they call a modern education. Just as soon as he is old enough and well enough they intend to send him on a tour around the world in charge of his tutor. He will visit the United

The Imperial Family

States, and then the several countries of Europe, returning by way of India and China.

The young prince has a palace and full establishment of his own, not far distant from that of the emperor and within the same walls. It is in charge of a grand chamberlain, the Marquis Nokayama, and three assistants, and an annual allowance of 50,000 yen, or half as much as the president of the United States receives, is appropriated by parliament to pay the young chap's expenses and maintain him with a dignity becoming the future Emperor of Japan. His separation from his father's establishment occurred when he was fifteen years old, and the organization is just as distinct and independent as if he were living in another country. He has a gymnasium, a bowling alley, tennis and archery courts, a riding pavilion, a shooting gallery and everything else that can be suggested for his improvement or his entertainment. His associates are his cousins and uncles belonging to the imperial family, who come and go at pleasure, and the sons of other princes and the nobles of the court. In former years he usually accompanied his father on all occasions of ceremony, especially when he reviewed the troops, and the neat little figure of his imperial highness became familiar to the people of Tokyo. He had ponies of his own, which he always rode when he went out formally, but was frequently carried to school

The Yankees of the East

in a jinrikisha. Since his illness very little is seen of him by the public. He has almost entirely disappeared, which suggests that his condition may be more serious than is generally supposed. If he were a well boy there would be no occasion for so much mystery or seclusion.

Few people believe that he will ever occupy the throne. It is the popular opinion that the next Mikado will be Prince Arisugawa, a second cousin of the emperor and a son of Prince Arisugawa Takahito, whose father was a younger brother of the emperor's father. Arisugawa is a little older than the prince imperial, and was adopted by the emperor as his own son in 1878 by the advice of the privy council after the death of the first heir-apparent, lest the government might be without a formally selected successor to the throne. When the present prince imperial was born, Arisugawa was dispossessed of that rank, although he remained an adopted son of the emperor and will undoubtedly be named in case the present prince imperial should die.

His mother is Princess Yasuko, daughter of an ex-daimyo, and his father is one of the best known and most progressive of the Japanese princes. He was educated in England and Germany, and has been to Europe twice for several years at a time. In 1887 he represented the Emperor of Japan at the jubilee of Queen Victoria. By hereditary rank he is the nominal conductor

The Imperial Family

of divine service for the imperial family under the Shinto regulations and custodian of the precious relics, the mirror, the crystal and the sword, which are said to have been handed down from Jimmu Tenno, the founder of the present dynasty, 660 B.C., to the present emperor, who is No. 122. At the same time he is a captain in the imperial navy and also saw active service in command of a cruiser in the late war with China. He resides in a palace just outside the castle grounds in Tokyo, and very near the United States legation. His house is of modern construction and is arranged partly upon the European and partly upon the Japanese plan. He is exceedingly democratic in his ideas and manners, plays poker, drives a fast horse, takes New York and London illustrated papers and magazines, is president of a club, gives dinner parties, garden parties and balls upon the Amercan plan, wears a suit of tweed and a polo cap when he rides horseback, and comes to the club after dinner in a Tuxedo suit, with diamond shirt-studs and low-cut patent leather shoes. It will thus be seen that he is thoroughly modernized, and his son, who may be the next emperor, is being brought up in the same atmosphere. He has an allowance of 30,000 yen a year from the government as well as a large private fortune.

There are eight other branches of the imperial family. Prince Komatsu, an uncle of the

The Yankees of the East

emperor, who was born in 1846, is commander-in-chief of the army. He also was educated in England and Germany and went to the jubilee of Queen Victoria as a representative of his nephew, the Mikado. His manners and ideas are quite as much modernized as those of Arisugawa. He commanded the Japanese army in the field during the recent war and is president of the Red Cross society. His salary is 22,500 yen.

Prince Fushima, another cousin of the emperor, is also a soldier, a major-general of the imperial guard, and commanded a division in the late war.

Prince Koto Hito, another cousin, who was born in 1865, is a captain of cavalry on the staff of Prince Komatsu.

Prince Akira, an adopted brother of the emperor, was educated in Germany. Very little is known of him. He lives a quiet, exclusive life.

Prince Yoshihisha, an uncle of the emperor, is a very different sort of person and takes an active interest in all outside affairs. He is particularly devoted to the industrial development of the country, takes shares in new factories and assists in the organization of new railroad enterprises. He is said to be one of the best posted men on the industrial arts of Japan and has been the active promoter and president of the exposi-

The Imperial Family

tions that were held in 1880, 1890 and 1895. He went down to Kyoto to present diplomas to successful exhibitors at the last summer's exposition. He has traveled a great deal in Europe and the United States and spent from 1870 to 1877 in England studying. He is president of the Imperial Geographical society and the Asiatic society of Japan and is a member of many of the learned societies of Europe. He has a degree from one of the English universities of which he is very proud. The faculty of the Imperial university at Tokyo usually make him the president of their examining board every year. He has an annual allowance of 20,000 yen from the government.

Prince Hiroyasu and Prince Morimasa, both cousins of the emperor, were educated in Germany and are progressive young men.

The lady members of the imperial circle are equally advanced in their ideas, and the whole court is pervaded by an atmosphere of culture. The grand master of ceremonies at the palace, who is the actual leader of society, has a German woman of noble birth for his wife. Many Japanese ladies have spent years in foreign countries and have acquired a modern education either in the schools of Europe and America or while residing at European capitals with their husbands in a diplomatic capacity.

Mme. Mutsu, wife of the minister of foreign

The Yankees of the East

affairs, lived four years in Washington, and was a great favorite there, and nearly every man and woman in the imperial circle except the emperor and empress has traveled or resided abroad. They all wear European dress, except in the privacy of their own apartments, follow European customs and etiquette, have French and Swiss cooks, butlers and other servants in livery similar to those of the English nobility. Their dinner parties and balls are conducted after the European fashion, although the Japanese, I fear, will never be able to dance as gracefully as their European sisters. They go through the figures with exceeding stiffness and serious formality, and, although perhaps it ought not to be mentioned, the Japanese woman invariably toes in. They look much better in their native costumes, too. The European dressmakers somehow or another do not fit them.

The beauty of the Japanese court is the Princess Kita-Shirakawa, who is tall, stately and graceful, and would rank well for looks among European women. Her husband is a cousin of the emperor, and a major-general in the imperial army. He is now in Formosa, where he has command of a corps.

The Princess Komatsu is also famous for her beauty although she is not considered so handsome as the Princess Kita. Her husband is also a cousin of the emperor, and is commander of

The Imperial Family

the imperial bodyguard. She is, perhaps, the most intimate friend the empress has among the ladies of the court, and usually accompanies her on occasions of ceremony. She also assists her majesty in looking after the many institutions which it is her pleasure to patronize. The Princess Komatsu is president of the Red Cross society, and as such takes an active interest in the medical and hospital corps of the army, and the hospitals in the city of Tokyo, where she lives. During the recent war she developed great executive ability in directing the affairs of the Red Cross society, and devoted her entire time to its organization and management. She speaks both French and English fluently.

In September, 1884, when the Japanese army embarked for China, the emperor went to Hiroshima, one of the most easterly ports of the inland sea, so that he might be 700 miles nearer the seat of war and communicate more conveniently with his officers. There is an impression, among the natives, which is not shared, however, by the foreigners, that his majesty took personal direction of the movements of the army, and that he at one time had an intention of exposing his sacred person to the hardships and dangers of the field. But, however this may have been, he remained at Hiroshima until June, 1895, when he returned to Tokyo attended by a great demonstration, in which all parties and factions and

The Yankees of the East

all classes of people joined with equal enthusiasm. He came first to Kyoto, which is the ancient capital, by sea, and hence by rail, stopping off for the night, starting early in the morning and reaching Tokyo at 2 o'clock sharp, the advertised time to the exact moment, which is not usually expected of royalty.

In 1892 I spent several days in the train of the Queen of Spain during a series of functions in honor of Christopher Columbus, and she was always three or four hours behindhand, whether it was a mass at the cathedral, a dinner at the palace or a ceremonial reception. Her majesty's subjects were expected always to be on time, but she came when she got ready, and several times she did not come at all. But in his movements on such occasions the Mikado has been a ideal of punctuality, and I am told that he usually sets a good example to his subjects by the practice of that virtue.

The Japanese are masters of the decorative art, and their taste and skill were most lavishly displayed in adornment, not only on the buildings and streets of the cities but in the groves and farms and paddy fields along the line of the railway. The distance from Yokohama, the principal seaport, to Tokyo, the capital, is eighteen miles, and almost the entire distance, on both sides of the track, was a continuous display of bunting and garlands of green. The railway

"THE BUND," YOKOHAMA.

The Imperial Family

stations, the switch houses and the telegraph poles were laden with color, and where the highways cross the track arches of cryptomaria—a sort of soft-leaved fir—were erected and inscribed with white designs representing the emperor's initials, the chrysanthemum, which is his crest, words of welcome and pledges of loyalty. In the bunting only the national colors were used—red and white—but there were a great many large white flags bearing inscriptions in Japanese characters, which are very decorative of themselves.

And from one city to the other the entire population were gathered along the hedges and fences that separate the railway right-of-way from the little toy farms, so that his majesty actually passed between two solid walls of his subjects for at least eighteen miles. And he was received with absolute silence, which seemed strange to us westerners, for until recently the emperor has never been cheered. The Japanese, who do almost everything in a manner the opposite to what we are accustomed, have always considered silence the highest form of respect. But after his train had passed out of hearing their pent-up emotions found relief in shouts and caperings, the waving of handkerchiefs and the flaunting of flags.

When he reached Tokyo, however, where the people have acquired modern ideas, there was a

The Yankees of the East

shout of welcome that came from 100,000 throats. It was the single word "Banzai!" which means literally "Ten thousand years!" and is used as an equivalent for the old salute that you read of in the scriptures, when subjects shouted to their sovereign: "Oh, king, live forever!"

Nor is it proper to look down upon the sacred person of the Mikado. You must always look up to him. Therefore the upper windows of the houses on the streets through which he passed were closed and curtained. There might have been some peeking from behind, but it was the height of disrespect.

The train stopped long enough at Yokohama for a brief and rather interesting ceremony. The city was decorated from one end to the other. Going through the principal streets one had to pass under arches of flags and through almost endless lines of lanterns of red and white paper and of grotesque shapes, which were all illuminated in the evening. The railway station was handsomely decorated, and just outside of it, in what might be called the switching yard, an inclosure had been arranged in which the ceremonies of welcome took place. The expense of the decoration was met by popular subscriptions. Each person who paid $1 was given a medal of brass bearing the emperor's name, the date and an inscription denoting the occasion. Only those who wore such medals were admitted

The Imperial Family

to the inclosure to witness the ceremony, and the natives could procure them at the city hall upon the payment of the subscription. Those who wanted to pay a little more could get medals of silver, and those who were very liberal could get them of gold. Foreigners were not invited to participate, and several Europeans were refused medals. But any American citizen could get one if he liked.

The antipathy of the people toward Europeans is illustrated by a little incident. A gentleman stopping at the Grand hotel went down to the headquarters of the committee at the city hall, and throwing down his dollar asked for a medal, which was refused him.

"No foreigner; no Englishman; he can't come," said the man in charge. "Only Japanese."

"I am not an Englishman," was the reply. "I am an American."

"Oh! Melican, he all right," and he handed out one of the souvenirs.

The emperor, however, did not leave his car at Yokohama, but the mayor of the city read an address to the members of his escort, eulogizing his majesty and congratulating him upon the triumphant closing of the war. The minister of the imperial household replied in appropriate terms on behalf of the sovereign. A committee from the municipal council and the city assem-

The Yankees of the East

bly then tendered baskets of flowers, and finally the chairman of the reception committee presented a beautiful tray of lacquer work filled with cakes, which is the Japanese expression of hospitality. Accompanying the tray was a casket containing the visiting cards of the members of the committee and the city government.

Drawn up around this inclosure were thousands of children from the public schools, each carrying a little flag and wearing a badge upon which was printed a greeting to the emperor. As the train entered and left the station they sang patriotic songs. There were also present various commercial and other civic organizations, each under its own banner.

The decorations at Tokyo were more elaborate, and there were three arches of evergreen which surpassed in magnificence anything I have ever seen. The railway station was effectively decorated with garlands, wreaths and bunting, while in front of it was an arch 200 feet wide at the base and 80 feet high. It was made of cryptomaria branches, covering a framework of timber, while on both sides were worked, in red and white, the imperial chrysanthemum and inscriptions of welcome. Another arch of similar design was erected in front of the entrance to the palace grounds, but the third, that stood opposite the houses of parliament, surpassed them all.

The Imperial Family

It consisted of a colonnade of arches each seventy feet span and seventy feet in height, the entire structure being 300 yards from end to end. At each end was a castellated tower, and in the center a dome of green 100 feet in height surmounted by the national colors. While the effect in the daylight was very impressive, at night it was much heightened by the glow of 1,500 colored electric lights arranged along the edges in the form of a border, and on the sides in the emperor's crest and the initials of his name.

The public buildings were handsomely decorated, as were the private dwellings, while the business streets were most liberally adorned with flags, banners and lanterns of every possible design and bearing innumerable inscriptions. The shipping in the bay was alive with banners, and just before reaching the city, where the railway skirts the shore, 1,000 or more sam-pans were drawn up in line and lashed together. They were covered with most ingenious designs and crowded with people. In a little plaza near the railway station was a large miniature ship of war, and in every direction through miles and miles of streets were designs of great originality and artistic skill.

And the masses of people that thronged the streets and the parks and parade grounds! Tokyo has 1,300,000 people and there are probably 10,000,000 within a radius of fifty miles.

The Yankees of the East

Shimosa and Musachi, the two southeastern provinces of Japan, are among the most densely peopled parts of the earth, and it seemed as if the whole population was there. The wide streets were filled from wall to wall with a dense stream of humanity slowly moving along, with here and there one of those exaggerated baby carriages they call jinrikishas, of which there are 30,000 in Tokyo. And there was never a more good-natured or a happier throng. Everybody was laughing and shouting, and some witticism or accident would occasionally cause a shout in which everybody participated. There was no drunkenness, no quarreling, no rudeness. This is the invariable characteristic of a Japanese crowd. They are altogether the happiest people in the world. Amusement is universal. Everybody laughs. Japan has been called the kingdom of merry dreams. It is equally the kingdom of merry wakefulness.

The nobles and other social and political swells all wore stovepipe hats and dress suits, and some of them were most comical caricatures. The silk hat is worn in Japan only on the most solemn occasions—weddings, funerals and royal ceremonies—and every man who pretends to be anybody keeps one in stock. As he never wears it out the same hat not only lasts a lifetime but is handed down from generation to generation, like the Mikado's crown. Many of

The Imperial Family

those on the street that merry day were evidently brought over soon after Commodore Perry came, and the rest must have come in installments since 1853, for they represented every fashion of headgear since that date.

As I have said, the emperor arrived promptly on time. His train was due at the Tokyo station at 2 o'clock. Five minutes later he was seated in the imperial carriage listening to the songs of thousands of school children, who had been gathered in front of the railway station to greet him. Then he was driven rapidly through the principal streets and parks of the city to the palace, preceded and followed by an escort of lancers, who rode stumpy little horses in a most awkward manner.

The line of march was roped off on either side of the roadway and patrolled by thousands of policemen. Behind the rope was a solid mass of people the entire distance, and scarcely a house or a shop was without some handsome decoration of foliage or bunting. At various points along the road were groups of priests in gorgeous robes, as well as organized societies of merchants and professional men.

His majesty's carriage was an open brougham with a gilt cloth over the coachman's box and the coat-of-arms of Japan upon the panels. It was drawn by two large black horses, whose harness was ornamented in simple designs of gold.

The Yankees of the East

The coachman and footman wore European livies, with silk stockings and breeches, tall hats with deep bands of gold and cockades of red and white, the national colors. Their coats were of blue broadcloth, with wide cuffs and collars of gold braid. In the carriage with his majesty was Count Tokudaiji, grand chamberlain of the palace. The emperor wore the uniform of a field marshal, and kept his eyes upon the buttons of his coachman's coat, looking neither to the right hand nor to the left.

Immediately following him, and alone in his carriage, was Count Ito, the prime minister, a solemn-faced man with long whiskers. Then came Prince Komatsu, an uncle of the emperor, who is commander-in-chief of the army, and was generalissimo of the forces in China, and several other high officials of the government and military men, including Count Mutsu, who used to be minister to Washington and left a sick-bed to meet his imperial master. Several members of the diplomatic corps were also at the railway station, and followed the procession to the palace, among them the Russian minister, whose carriage was surrounded by detectives, and for that reason attracted more than ordinary attention. He seemed to have made himself as conspicuous as possible, owing to the strained relations between his country and the Japanese, and

The Imperial Family

was greeted with groans and hoots of derision as he passed through the streets.

During the evening the city was illuminated in a most gorgeous manner. Millions of lanterns were tossed in the breeze and thousands of houses and buildings were blazing with electric lights. In all the parks and public squares and at many private entertainments were elaborate displays of fireworks until the air of the whole city was laden with the odor of powder.

What was most interesting of all was that these demonstrations are genuine and sincere. No matter how bitterly the politicians may abuse each other, nor how stubborn the opposition may be to the policy of the government, the loyalty of all classes to their emperor is unquestionable, and the common people still consider Mutsu Hito as a sacred personage who will become a divinity when he dies.

It is a remarkable fact concerning the day of the emperor's reception at Tokyo, when all the population of a city of 1,300,000 people were out to greet him and 500,000 strangers were brought in by the railroads from the surrounding country, that, according to the Yomiuri Shimbun (News), no person was arrested, or robbed, or injured; no child was lost; there were no quarrels of sufficient seriousness to require the intervention of the police, and the only accident reported for the entire day was the collision of

The Yankees of the East

three jinrikishas, which were racing to the railway station and were all trying to cross a narrow bridge at the same time. It has often been said that the Japanese are the best-natured and the most orderly people in the world, and the demonstration in honor of their emperor was a good test of these qualities.

The empress went from Kyoto to Tokyo one day behind the emperor. The same decorations and committees, like the same itinerary, fitted both. It was only necessary for the government to furnish another train and for the populace at the points she visited to provide a new set of souvenirs.

The imperial couple never travel together. I asked an explanation from several people who have lived there a long time, and from certain Japanese gentlemen who are well up in etiquette, but none of them was very positive in his opinion. Most of them said that there was no particular reason; that it was merely one of the customs of the country inherited from ancient times. Others explained that the empress was an inferior being, and that it would not be according to the traditional ideas of the emperor's superhuman attributes to admit his wife to an equality; but these oriental customs and traditions are too complicated to waste time over them. The more you study them the more confused you get.

The Imperial Family

Her imperial majesty was much more gracious, however, than her husband. He did not leave his car from one end of the journey to the other, and was represented by the minister of the imperial household at all the functions on the road. She came several times to the platforms that were erected for reception ceremonies and received memorials in writing, bouquets, trays of cakes, which signify hospitality, and caskets containing the visiting cards of the reception committees, but all the speeches were made in her behalf by the grand master of ceremonies. But she smiled and bowed and waved her hand at the people, and at Yokohama she asked that the ropes which surrounded the platform might be taken away, so that the people could come nearer to her. As a measure of precaution the police had roped off an area about one hundred yards square to accommodate fifty or sixty dignitaries.

Several times on the journey her majesty came out on the platform of the car and smiled and bowed to the crowds that were assembled together, and afforded them an immense amount of gratification, for it isn't often that a Japanese peasant has an opportunity to look at a queen. She was dressed in a delicate mauve gown, made in Paris, with a bonnet to match, which was quite gay for a traveling costume, and all the ladies of her escort wore foreign fashions. Not

The Yankees of the East

a person in the entire cortege appeared in the native dress. The servants were in livery, the ladies in waiting, of whom there were a dozen or more, wore gowns of light colors and light gloves, more suitable for a lawn party than a railway journey, while the men folk that did not have uniforms wore dress suits of black broadcloth, white gloves and most ridiculous silk hats.

The same school children and guilds of professional and commercial men that received the emperor on the day previous sung the same songs and presented similar testimonials to the imperial consort, and although the crowd was not so large either at Tokyo or Yokohama it was equally enthusiastic and shouted "Banzai!" quite as ardently.

One of the local papers said:

"It is noticeable that now for the first time have Japanese crowds begun to open their lungs as the sovereign passes. The most complete silence, decorous and reverential, used invariably to be preserved, but bursts of cheering have at last become the rule as in other countries. "Banzai!" is an excellent form of shout. It has a fine full sound, and a man finds no difficulty in putting his whole soul into it. But though the people have readily adopted this innovation from the West, the emperor and empress still retain the traditional attitude of dignified calm. Throughout the drive from the train to the palace each of the imperial personages obeyed the same rule, gazed steadily at the line of troops presenting arms, and took not the slightest notice of the cheering crowd."

The Imperial Family

This is all true except the last sentence, so far as it refers to the empress. She smiled and bowed to the shouting multitude as cordially and as gracefully as Mrs. Cleveland could have done, and seemed to enjoy the demonstrations. The imperial master of ceremonies, who sat upon the front seat of her carriage, frowned and looked very forbidding, but Haru Ko was as gracious as could be.

The empress has no imperial blood in her veins, but is the daughter of one of the five noblest families of the empire, for the laws of Japan, and wisely, I think, forbid the dilution of the vitality of their rulers by the marriage of relatives. The only destiny open to a princess is to marry some noble below her rank or go into a Shinto convent. Some of the nations of Europe might well adopt this custom and breed a stronger race of kings.

I suppose the time will come when the Mikado may look for a wife among the royal households of Europe, but at present his consorts—I speak in the plural—are selected for him by the imperial council. He is supposed to have nothing to say about it for himself, but has to accept the brides they bring him.

As Artemus Ward would have said, Mrs. Mutsu Hito is nine in number—one empress and eight imperial concubines, but the latter have no social rank and never appear on cere-

The Yankees of the East

monial occasions. They seem to be a sort of guaranty that there shall be an heir to the throne, as their children are recognized as of full standing in the royal pedigree, and the present heir-apparent is the son of one of them. They also are selected by the council from among the daughters of the first families in the land because of their pure blood, their health and beauty, and sometimes for political reasons, for it is considered the highest distinction that can be conferred upon a woman in Japan—to be empress is only nobler. The left-handed wives of the emperor often wield a tremendous political influence, for obvious reasons, and their relatives are supposed to profit thereby. They live in the greatest luxury, are surrounded by multitudes of attendants, and except for their omission in the court codes of etiquette, which do not provide for them, they stand equal to the empress herself.

Haru Ko, the empress, is the third daughter of the late Prince Ichijo Tadaka, who resided in Tokyo, and was a very highly respected gentleman, tracing back his ancestry through the Fujiwara family for a thousand years. Her name means "Springtime." She was born in 1850, and was married in 1869, when she was 19 years old and the emperor was only 17. He had just passed through the revolution which ended the tyranny of the tycoon, and had been

The Imperial Family

brought to the new capital at Tokyo as the recognized ruler of the people. Her father had been active in the struggle, and as he represented one of the largest and most influential families in Japan the selection of his daughter as a bride for the young Mikado was appropriate, and approved by the nation. She has never had children, which is a great disappointment to the people as well as to the emperor and herself.

The empress was brought up and educated in the old-fashioned way, which makes the readiness with which she adopted foreign manners and customs the more remarkable. Before her marriage she had been carefully trained in the old code of etiquette, and knew absolutely nothing of modern civilization, but when the restoration took place and foreign ideas came into fashion she was furnished with instructors and adapted herself with the greatest skill and grace to the new régime, so that in all things she is the actual as well as the nominal leader of the court. Although she takes no interest in politics she is largely engaged in benevolent and educational movements, and presided over the committee that arranged for the famous exhibit in the woman's building at the Columbian exposition. She appears frequently at ceremonial entertainments, at the openings of exhibitions, corner-stone layings, and the inauguration of public enterprises, garden parties, and that sort of

The Yankees of the East

thing, and conducts herself with quite as much dignity and grace as the remarkable woman who now presides at the White house in Washington.

At solemn court functions the emperor sits alone in a gilded chair upon a low platform under a canopy, as becomes a son of heaven who can count back his ancestors for 2,500 years. The empress sits upon a platform to the right, a little below the throne, surrounded by the rest of the imperial family. This recognition of women is the most striking feature of the late reformation. In former times the empress was only an inmate of the harem, secluded and excluded like the rest, but on February 11, 1889, the Mikado did two things which make him memorable among the greatest monarchs of history. He relinquished the autocratic power he had inherited from his ancestors, gave Japan a constitutional government, and for the first time the equality of women was recognized in his dominions.

It took some years for the empress to accustom herself to modern ideas. She stopped blacking her teeth and let her eyebrows grow immediately after her marriage, but it was not until 1886 that she discarded the kimono of her race and adopted the fashions of Paris, and even then the etiquette of the court forbade the vulgar hands of a dressmaker to touch the sacred person of an empress, so the wife of Count Ito, the prime minister, who is about her size and figure,

The Imperial Family

was used as a model for measuring and fitting her majesty's wardrobe. There was a solemn protest from both natives and foreigners against the abandonment of the artistic drapery of the Japanese for the stiff, conventional garments of Europe and America, but it was a matter of politics, and the council of ministers ordered that the Mikado's wife must set an example to her subjects in introducing "modern improvements." It was not until the adoption of the constitution, however, that she appeared in public in her Paris gowns, and even now she is said to wear the native costume in the privacy of her palace, for which one cannot blame her, as corsets and tight-fitting bodices must be very uncomfortable to one whose form grew in nature's mold under the loose kimono.

The empress is supposed to speak English, but she never does. When addressed in English by ladies who have been permitted to approach her she listens and smiles and keeps silent. She is a tiny little thing, delicate and slender, about as large as the ordinary girl of 10 years in America. She has a long, thin face, with the Japanese eyes, pointed chin and flat features, and conceals her natural complexion and the color of her lips by the use of native cosmetics which do not embellish beauty.

I suppose I should say that she is beautiful and graceful and all that, but she isn't if one

The Yankees of the East

judge by the classic types. No Japanese woman looks well in a modern costume, not even an empress.

The private affairs of the emperor are managed by the minister of the household. He occupies a fine building of French architecture near the entrance to the palace grounds, with a large staff of secretaries and assistants. It takes a great many men and a great deal of money to look after the welfare of the Mikado, but most of their time is taken up by the almost ceaseless ceremony that has been inherited from ancient times. Occasionally they lop off a nonsensical formality that was introduced to gratify the vanity of some prince or please some Mikado, but there is still plenty of it left, and between the devotion he pays to the dead and the devotion he receives from the living Mutsu Hito has a pretty busy time.

As an example, he is the one hundred and twenty-second emperor of his line, and each of his predecessors has a birthday or some other anniversary upon which his memory must be honored by worship before the tablets that bear his names and important statistical information.

A bureau of ritual composed of ten laymen and a number of Shinto priests, who are mostly members of the imperial family or related to the emperor in some way, assist him in his religious duties and often worship his ancestors in his

THE WALL OF THE IMPERIAL PALACE, TOKYO.

The Imperial Family

place when he has something more important to do. They keep watch of the calendar, and when the birthday of some particular ancestor arrives, and often two were born on the same date— which was very kind of them and saves quite a good deal of the imperial time—their tablets are brought out from the handsome lacquer boxes and brocade wrappings in which they are preserved and placed upon a shrine in the palace with bowls of rice and other food, cups of saké, fresh flowers appropriate to the season, foliage plants and other ornaments that belong to the outfit of the particular person who is to be worshiped. At a certain hour in the day, with great pomp and ceremony, the emperor appears at the head of a procession of princes and priests, and prays for the assistance and blessing of that particular ancestor, who has been deified and now lives among the gods, able to exercise an influence for good or for evil over the affairs of mortals.

If any misfortune overtakes the state or if anything happens to the emperor it is usually attributed to his neglect of his religious duties, and those who attend to such affairs endeavor to trace back the difficulty to the evil influence of some neglected ancestor.

The ancestral tablet is a rather insignificant looking affair, being a piece of wood about eight inches long and three inches wide mortised into

The Yankees of the East

a little pedestal that is usually beautifully carved and gilded. The tablet itself often bears ornaments of gold, but is usually covered with plain black lacquer and the necessary lettering in gold. Every man who dies is given a posthumous name under which he is deified, and it usually has reference to some of his achievements while living.

While the bureau of ritual looks after the religious duties of the Mikado, the bureau of ceremonies, which consists of a grand master and twenty assistants, mostly marquises, counts and viscounts, attends to formalities that relate to the living, and theirs is a very delicate and perplexing duty. They arrange for all dinners and receptions, for public and private audiences, teas, garden parties and balls, and as everything is done by rote and the etiquette is very exacting, it requires a great deal of time and attention to arrange the daily programme for the Mikado and get in and out of the palace in a proper manner the people that his imperial majesty has to see.

The empress has her own establishment, entirely separate and distinct, her own privy purse, chamberlain and stewards, and is just as independent of the rest of the royal family as if she were alone in the world. The same is true of the empress-dowager, the mother of his majesty, who lives outside the palace grounds in a beautiful chateau that is screened from observation by a miniature forest and tall yellow walls. The

The Imperial Family

eight concubines of the emperor live in a detached palace connected with the emperor's residence by an arcade. Each has her separate suite of apartments, her maids and other attendants, and the whole are under the control of one of the nine chamberlains of the imperial household. But very little is known of them, and they all might die and be buried and turn to dust without the public being any the wiser.

There is a bureau of music, a bureau of decorations, a bureau of finance, which supervises the expenditure of the $3,000,000 which is appropriated annually by parliament for the expenses of the imperial household; a bureau of palace keepers, who look after the thirty palaces that belong to the imperial family in different parts of the empire, as well as those in which the Mikado lives at Tokyo and Kyoto, and a bureau of the imperial estates, which attends to the management of the private property of the emperor, for he has farms, forests, factories, real estate of various kinds, and other investments, like any gentleman, although I presume he knows very little about them. There is also a bureau of construction and repairs, a bureau of provisions and cookery and a bureau of hunting, which sees that the game preserves that belong to the crown are not poached upon. The emperor never went hunting in his life, but he might want to do so, and if everything wasn't

The Yankees of the East

ready for him, with plenty of deer, stags, boars, pheasants and other wild birds and beasts, there would be a tremendous scandal.

The imperial stables have a bureau to look after them; also the imperial tombs and the imperial library and private records. There is a museum attached to the palace which requires the attention of several learned pundits, and a large collection of antiquities that have descended from one generation of emperors to another, including ceremonial gowns, swords, armor and wardrobes, and they all have to be dusted and inspected occasionally by men appointed especially for that purpose. The palace police and fire department are managed by a marquis, who is held responsible for the safety of the imperial property, and a bureau of medicine, consisting of fourteen native physicians, looks after the health of the family and all those who attend at the palace. There is also a commission of venerable nobles whose sole duty is to protect the privy seal, which is the most sacred thing about the palace except the person of the emperor himself, and cannot be attached to any document except in the presence of two or more of its custodians, who record the fact and the circumstances in a big book kept for that purpose.

Each of these bureaus is under the direction of a president, who is either a prince, a marquis,

GATEWAY TO THE IMPERIAL PALACE, TOKYO.

The Imperial Family

or a count, and although one would judge from my description that their duties must be light, they make a great deal of hard work in performing them.

There are thirty palaces belonging to the imperial family in various parts of the country, but the present emperor has never occupied more than three or four of them, and some of them he has never seen. The emperor seldom leaves the new palaces at Tokyo, which are more modern and comfortable than any of the others, and were only completed in 1888. They consist of a labyrinth of one-story buildings, all connected by covered passages and surrounding beautiful courts. Their architecture is of the ancient Japanese style, with high roofs at sharp angles and heavy gray tiles, and the interior of most of them is finished in the native fashion, with partitions of sliding screens and floor matting, which the inmates use for beds, chairs and tables, as it happens to be necessary. But several of the rooms have French furniture of ornate and expensive workmanship, much of it being rosewood handsomely carved and inlaid. The apartments occupied by the emperor and empress are furnished in that way. Both prefer to sleep in a modern bed and sit on a chair before a table, with knives and forks and china, when they take their meals.

Built upon uneven ground and separated by

long covered corridors that may be cut away in case of a fire, one is continually going up and down stairs and through dark passages when he visits the palace, and it seems strange to see steam heat and electric lights in apartments that are separated by gilded screens and lighted by paper windows.

The state dining-room is very Frenchy. The walls are covered with oil paintings, the several mantels with gilt clocks, and the sideboards with china and crystal that resemble what you see in the Chicago shops. The ballroom has a costly inlaid floor and is decorated in white and gold. The throneroom, which is used only on occasions of the greatest ceremony, has an inlaid floor, handsome chandeliers of European manufacture, window hangings of exquisite Japanese brocade and a paneled ceiling ornamented with the imperial crest. The throne is a large armchair, handsomely carved and gilded, standing upon a platform that is covered with a red rug and under a canopy of red plush with gold fringe and tassels.

The emperor has a suite of private apartments, consisting of libraries, studies, smoking and dressing-rooms, which are finished in the Japanese style with unpainted woodwork, paper windows and sliding screens, but the floors are covered with moquette carpets and the furniture was all imported from France. He also has a

The Imperial Family

fireplace, the only one in the palace, in which pine wood is burned, but his sleeping-room is the same unventilated, unlighted and unattractive closet that his ancestors used. It stands in the center of a group of rooms which are always occupied at night by his bodyguard, so that the

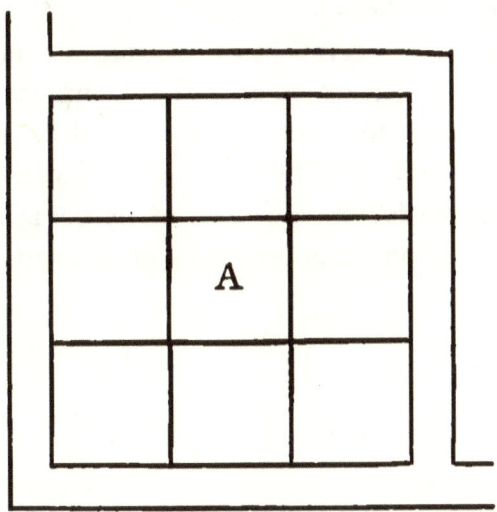

LOCATION OF THE EMPEROR'S BEDROOM.

imperial person cannot be approached from any direction without an alarm being given. There are nine square apartments, as shown in the accompanying diagram, and the emperor's French bed is erected in the central one, marked "A." The guards in the other rooms are specially selected for their bravery and fidelity, and are descendants of those who performed a similar duty for previous sovereigns.

The Yankees of the East

All the formal banquets, breakfasts and luncheons given at the palace are served in foreign style, except a breakfast which the emperor gives on his birthday to the members of the imperial family—his uncles and his cousins and his aunts. Then chop-sticks and lacquer bowls are used for the native food, and saké, the native drink, is served in little cups, as small and as thin as an eggshell. The empress often gives a ceremonial tea, the famous rite of Cha-no-yu, to her favorites among the ladies of the court, more for the purpose of perpetuating an ancient custom than for social enjoyment.

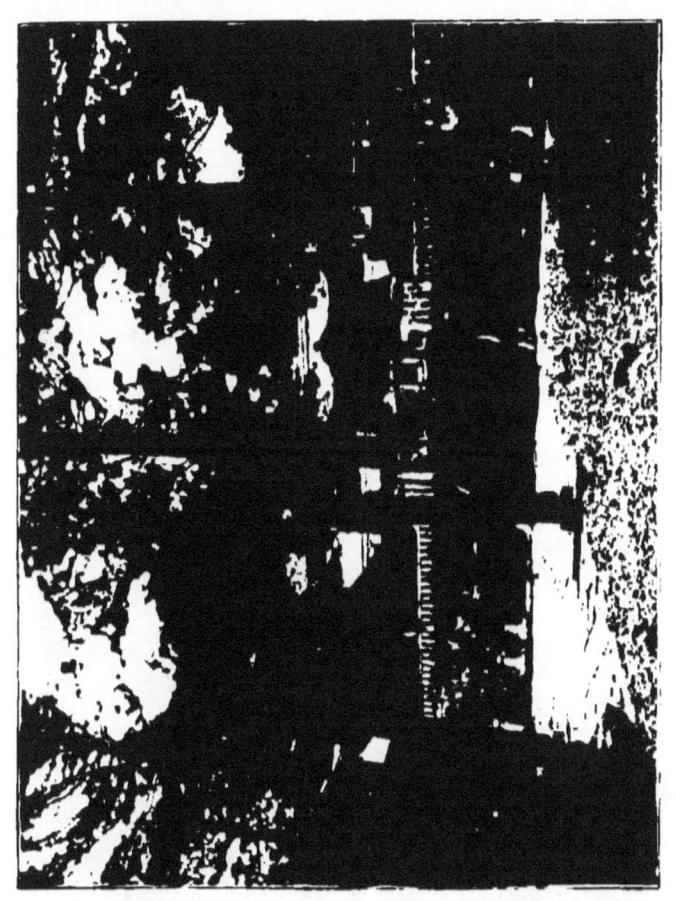

APPROACH TO THE GREAT TEMPLES AT NIKKO.

IV

The Tycoon in Seclusion

In the last half of the sixteenth century, during a period of anarchy, a great man appeared in Japan—the greatest in the history of the empire. He came from the samurai or military class; he was a soldier of fortune; his name was Tokugawa Ieyasu, and he founded a dynasty which continued to rule the empire for more than 250 years in profound peace. It was the golden age in Japan. Nagasaki was the only place in the empire at which intercourse with foreigners was permitted, and no nation but the Dutch were allowed to trade even there until 1853, when the government of the United States, through Commodore Perry, broke down the policy of isolation. When it fell the whole structure of mediæval feudalism collapsed. The shogunate was abolished. The emperor emerged from his enforced seclusion and was restored to actual power.

But the Tycoon Ieyasu was not the author of the policy of isolation. He was a broad-minded, wise and progressive man. He was to Japan

The Yankees of the East

what Peter the Great was to Russia, Frederick the Great to Prussia and Charlemagne to France. He was not only a soldier, but a statesman, a law-giver and a patron of the arts and sciences. His code of 100 laws, by which Japan was governed for nearly three centuries, was worthy of Solon himself, and to him was due the development of Japanese art, industry and literature.

Ieyasu worked his way up from the ranks to the command of the army, until in 1603 he exacted from the emperor the title of shogun, or tycoon (literally "general-in-chief"), grasped all the power of the government in his own hands and placed the Mikado upon a secluded pedestal behind the golden doors of the palace at Kyoto. The people worshiped him as a divinity, while Ieyasu and his successors reigned as regents in his name. Ieyasu built powerful strongholds and established arsenals, constructed a system of admirable highways throughout the country, introduced a postal service and promulgated laws which, if the theory of paternal government may be approved, were the best in use on the continent of Asia and in most of the countries of Europe at his time. It was his grandson, Iemitsu, the third shogun of the Tokugawa dynasty, who suppressed Christianity, closed the country against foreigners and forbade his own subjects to go abroad. He perfected the system of government which his

THE SACRED BRIDGE AT NIKKO.

The Tycoon in Seclusion

grandfather established, but was not so able nor so wise a man.

The tomb of Ieyasu at Nikko is the most splendid piece of architecture in the East. In accordance with the Shinto faith the Japanese worship him as a god under the name of Tosho-gu (the general who illuminated the east) in allusion to the fact that his greatest glory was accomplished in eastern Japan. The series of magnificent temples at Nikko are nearly all dedicated to Ieyasu and his grandson Iemitsu, and there is nothing in all the world to compare with them for carving, gilding and other decorative work. Nikko is the most sacred of all the sacred places of Japan. It lies in a narrow valley, walled in by a range of sacred mountains still covered with primeval forests, and legend has peopled them with impossible beings—demons and dragons, giants and gnomes, fairies and elfins. It is like the Black forest of Germany in the mythology of the people, and the scenes of most of the fairy stories in the literature of the country are laid there.

With its vast groves of majestic trees shading broad avenues and staircases, its imposing temples, monasteries and palaces, Nikko has a strange fascination for the stranger, and its calm, serious air attracts pilgrims, poets, scholars, artists and all who love the picturesque to rest and reflect awhile among the sacred groves.

The Yankees of the East

Everything is old and moss-grown, except the gold and red lacquer that adorns the temples, and all the splendid paths lead to two great sanctuaries in which the bones of Ieyasu and Iemitsu lie. No nation could pay a higher tribute to its great men.

The early and the latter days of Ieyasu were spent at Shizuoka, where he was educated at a Buddhist temple called Rin-dai-ji (literally, wood-great-temple), and its roof still shelters precious relics of his youth and manhood and old age. His saddles and swords, the camp equipage he carried in war, the garments he wore on ceremonial occasions and his military dress, many books that contain his writings, including an autograph letter from one of the Mikados, and even some specimen fossils that he once collected, are preserved with religious care and exhibited with reverence. We were shown the rooms in which he lived during his old age, and a plum tree that he planted shortly before his death, which is now gnarled and hoary, surrounded by a fence to protect it and propped up by supports. On the other side of the temple is a little pine tree that was planted by the present crown prince in 1894.

The successors of Ieyasu came here at certain times of the year to worship their ancestor, and when Hitosu-Bashi, the last of the tycoons, was overthrown in 1868, he retired to the old

The Tycoon in Seclusion

family estate, and has spent the years of reform in the strictest seclusion. He has left the place but once, and that was when his wife died in Tokyo in 1893, and he never admits any one to his presence, not even the nobles that once composed his court. The only persons he will see are members of the imperial family, who sometimes come to Shizuoka, and nine of his old retainers who have remained faithful to him and afford him companionship in his solitude.

His residence is in the center of a park about as large as six or seven city blocks and is surrounded by a hedge and a high black wooden fence. It lies on the edge of Shizuoka, where the houses and the ricefields meet, only a few hundred yards from the old temple at which his ancestor was educated. Shizuoka is in the heart of the tea country, and from any street corner a beautiful view of Fujiyama, the sacred volcano, can be obtained.

We thought perhaps even a dethroned shogun might admit a party of pilgrims to his presence, so we stopped off at Shizuoka while on our way to Kyoto and took jinrikishas to his palace. A stately looking attendant stopped us at the porter's lodge and asked our business. The interpreter explained that three Americans, one of them an officer in the United States army, desired to pay their respects to the shogun, and handed him our cards. A dignified smile encir-

The Yankees of the East

cled his lips as he looked us over, and he replied politely that, although he feared his highness would decline to see us, as he did everybody else, he would be glad to carry our cards and our message to him. In the meantime he invited us out of the sun into the cool rooms of his cottage, where his wife and mother received us cordially and gossiped about the shogun as fast as their tongues could talk. They said he was sixty-six years old, has two wives living with him there and buried another two years before in Tokyo. He has twelve children, all of whom are residing in Tokyo except the three youngest, who are at home. Some of the children are grown up and married, others are receiving a modern education at what is known as the nobles' schools, where the children of princes and peers only are admitted. The prince hasn't been out of Shizuoka for nearly twenty-five years, except once two years ago, when his wife, who was visiting her son in Tokyo, was taken seriously ill and sent for him to come to her bedside.

A great many of his friends and admirers, the old dames said, always called and left their cards when they came to Shizuoka, but he never saw them. Once in a while one of the princes of the imperial family came down, whom he is compelled to admit out of respect to the emperor, but he never seeks their society. The crown

RECENT PORTRAIT OF THE EMPEROR.

The Tycoon in Seclusion

prince was there last spring and made a little visit, but when the emperor stopped off at Shizuoka on his way to the capital in June the shogun did not offer to entertain him, but let him go to a hotel. He did not even call upon his sovereign there; and has seen him but once since the restoration of 1868. That was while he was in Tokyo after the funeral of his wife. His majesty sent a letter of condolence and the etiquette of the country required him to acknowledge it by a personal call.

When we asked what his highness thought about the progress of Japan and the foreign ideas that were being adopted by everybody, they replied that he never discussed the subject, but he must be favorable to them because he always wore European dress when he went out, is educating his children in mödern schools where there are foreign instructors, takes foreign newspapers and other publications and buys many foreign books. He cannot read any language but his own, but often has French and English literature translated to him by his retainers.

For exercise his highness has an archery court within his grounds, rides horseback a great deal, and often hunts and fishes in the mountains around Shizuoka.

While we were thus gossiping the porter came back with a message that the major-domo desired to see our interpreter, and we thought the

The Yankees of the East

shogun had decided to admit us to his august presence, but Sano soon came back with an explanation that his highness only wanted to know who we were, and where we came from, and to have our cards translated into Japanese for him. The major-domo said the tycoon was very sorry to disappoint us, but made it a rule never to admit any one to his presence. He was living in absolute retirement and denied himself to all visitors.

The family of the shogun is active in public affairs, although he remains in seclusion, as a permanent protest, I suppose, against his overthrow and the innovations that have followed it. His oldest son stands at the head of the nobility, only one grade below the princes of the imperial house. He is known as Prince Tokugawa. He lives at Sendagaya, a suburb of Tokyo, and is an active member of the house of peers. He was educated in England, and spent seven years there and on the continent. The second son, the Marquis Tokugawa, was also educated abroad and speaks French and English fluently. He is vice-grand master of ceremonies at the imperial palace. A third son, Viscount Tokugawa, is a graduate of the Imperial university and has recently returned from an extended journey abroad. He is an enthusiastic devotee of photography and president of the Amateur society in Japan. The sons visit their father reg-

The Tycoon in Seclusion

ularly and manage his immense property for him. He has estates in several provinces of Japan, which were allowed to remain in his possession when what was considered public property was seized by the crown at the time of his overthrow.

In area, as well as in population, Tokyo is one of the largest cities in the world. It has more than 1,300,000 inhabitants and covers an area of 100 square miles. The old name was Yedo, so called in honor of one Yedo Taro Shigenaga, who built a castle in the wilderness on the banks of the bay in 1456; but the name was changed after the fall of the shogun in 1868, when the Mikado came there and took up his abode in the old palace. The meaning of the term Tokyo is "eastern capital," which has come into common use to distinguish it from Kyoto, which means "western capital." It stands at the head of Yedo Bay, about eighteen miles above Yokohama and thirty miles from the ocean.

At the time the fortress was built in the middle ages, most of the ground was occupied by lagoons, which have been dredged out and banked up with walls of stone, and form a system of canals which are very convenient for local transportation and are navigated by thousands of sampans—long, sharp-nosed boats propelled by one or two oars from the stern, after the manner of sculling. The military advantages of the

The Yankees of the East

place were recognized by the great Ieyasu, who was the actual founder of the city.

There is an interesting story in Japanese history which accounts for the exclusive policy adopted by the successors of the great shogun. It is said that a Jesuit priest once remarked to a Japanese noble with whom he was having a controversy:

"My master the pope will one day be the sovereign of the whole world."

"How can that be?" was asked.

"The church sends out missionaries who convert the nations," was the reply, "and when all the nations are converted to the faith of Rome, the pope will be the ruler of the world."

This boastful remark set the shogun thinking when it came to his ears, and recognizing that a million or more of his subjects had already accepted the Roman Catholic faith, he issued an edict expelling the Catholic missionaries from the empire, and forbidding the further worship of the Christian God. All Japanese who had joined the church were required to renounce it or suffer the penalty of banishment or death.

In the harbor of Nagasaki, at the extreme west of the empire across the Yellow sea from China, is a rock called *Tokaboko*, or Pappenberg, rising out of the ocean almost perpendicularly to the height of 200 feet. On the land side is a flight of stairs hewn in the solid rock. In 1620,

PAPPENBERG ISLAND, NAGASAKI HARBOR.

The Tycoon in Seclusion

only two weeks after the pilgrims landed at Plymouth, 10,000 Catholic converts were driven up those stairs, and when they reached the top of the rock were given their option between renouncing Christianity or plunging into the sea below. Between 2,000 and 3,000 recanted and were allowed to return to their homes. The rest, with the spirit of the early martyrs, remained steadfast to the faith and were driven off the edge of the precipice at the point of the spears of the tycoon's soldiers.

Much of the area of Tokyo is occupied by parks and temple grounds and the palace of the Mikado, which stands in the center of the city surrounded by a serpentine moat. The grounds of the palace have been much reduced in later years, but still cover twenty-six acres upon a noble hill, which is enclosed in massive walls and can be reached only by two bridges. No one is allowed to enter the gates except the higher officials of the government and those who are invited by the emperor. The latter bear passes issued by the minister of the household, and it is impossible for tourists to obtain them, because the emperor insists upon preserving his privacy, and if one person were favored it would be necessary to admit hundreds every week.

Very few of the people of Tokyo have ever been inside the castle gates. A prominent member of parliament and an active supporter of the

The Yankees of the East

present government, who was born in Tokyo and has spent his whole life there, told me he had never entered the grounds but once, and that was on the occasion of a garden party given to celebrate the birthday of the emperor. Very few persons who have not held high official positions have ever had a similar privilege.

When the shogun reigned he required all the feudal lords to spend six months of each year at the capital, and retained their families as hostages while they were absent. Each had his castle and barracks for his retainers, and at times the number of persons living within the enclosure exceeded 250,000.

But the castles of the daimyos have all been torn down, and the area they occupied is now devoted to public buildings, parks and parade grounds, which have to be crossed in passing from one portion of the city to another. Therefore, the distances are very great, and, as there is no division of the different classes of business, much time is spent in jinnrikishas or carriages driving back and forth.

The houses are nearly all wood, seldom more than two stories in height and the most of them are of a single story. They are very inflammable, and, as candles and kerosene are the chief means of light, fires are frequent. Like Constantinople, it is said that Tokyo is entirely burned over once in five years. But this is an

The Tycoon in Seclusion

exaggeration. There are fire engine houses at frequent intervals with steam engines of English manufacture, and tall towers rise above them in which watchmen are always looking out for smoke and flames. When they see signs of a fire they pound a large bell, and the fire department starts for the scene of the conflagration almost as promptly as ours at home. One of the assistant chiefs of the department told me that they were usually able to get up steam in three minutes, and that they had an average of eighty fires a month. But there is very little to burn in the ordinary Japanese house—simply the walls and the floor and the roof, for the partitions are only sliding screens, and there is no furniture except a few little low tables, cushions and mats.

Insurance premiums are high. On city property the usual rate is 2 per cent. There are some local insurance companies, but most of the business is done by native agents of European companies—English, German, French and Swiss. No United States insurance companies have offices in Japan, although I think it would be very profitable to open one. While the risk is greater than in our own country, where the buildings are less combustible, the local companies pay large dividends—16, 18 and often as high as 25 per cent.—and I suppose that foreign companies make an equal profit. A gentleman in Yokohama who represents a German

The Yankees of the East

insurance company told me that his receipts from premiums were about seven times as great as the losses paid.

Life insurance is not popular in Japan, which seems to be accounted for by a custom of the country which requires relatives to look after the families of the dead. For the same reasons there are no orphan asylums. There are plenty of hospitals for the sick and institutions for the education of the blind, the deaf and dumb and others afflicted in a similar manner, but when a man dies his widow goes back to the home of her parents or to that of her eldest brother and the children are divided around. If there is any property each has his share by division under the will, if there happens to be one, or by arbitration conducted after a novel plan. The father or the eldest brother becomes a trustee to manage the business or the property of the deceased for the benefit of his heirs until the eldest son is able to take charge. If there is no property the children are adopted into the families of relatives. There are no almshouses or homes for the indigent and beggars except priests are not often seen upon the streets. It costs but little for food, and no family is so poor that it cannot add another to the household, and the industry of the people is such that labor begins almost with birth and ends only with death.

The Tycoon in Seclusion

Each family has a chest made of hardwood, in which they keep their valuables and extra clothing, and it can be carried into the street in a moment whenever danger threatens. These chests are marvels of cabinetmaking. No nails or screws or iron of any kind are used in their construction except hinges and locks and bands to make them more secure, but the joints are mortised so skillfully that when closed they are water-tight and will float for hours in a river without the slightest injury to their contents.

Wealthier families, who have many valuables — fine silks, brocades, pictures, porcelain, cloisonné and other ornaments — always have what they call a "kura," a fireproof vault erected of solid masonry in the back yard, with heavy doors and shutters. The roof is of tiles and there is nothing about it that can burn. Whenever they want a change of clothing they go to the kura instead of a closet or a wardrobe. It is the custom of Japanese families, even the richest of them, to keep only one or two ornaments displayed for their own enjoyment and that of their visitors. The remainder of their works of art and bric-à-brac is stored away in the kura, and taken out piece by piece at intervals of a few days to replace those that have been in service.

The most precious heirlooms in every Japanese household are the swords that belonged to the ancestors of the family. In olden times

The Yankees of the East

every man was expected to have as many swords as he had garments, with a variety of sizes and makes, as well as blades, and when you visit one of the old families to-day they invariably exhibit for your admiration the weapons their ancestors wore.

A Japanese gentleman remarked that he thought the American and European plan of covering the walls of houses with pictures and other decorations was vulgar, for no man of taste could enjoy more than one work of art at a time. The Japanese, he said, enjoyed their treasures more than other people because they did not make them common, and never destroyed their novelty by frequent inspection. When you visit a rich Japanese he will send to the kura and have his choicest gems displayed for your inspection. They are usually inclosed in the daintiest of boxes and wrapped in cerements of cotton or silk. His pictures are hung on rolls called kakemonos. They are never framed under glass as ours are. The swords his ancestors wore in feudal times are incased in bags of wool or silk, and are brought out with the greatest degree of reverence; and before he puts them away the servants bathe them with oil of cloves and sprinkle them with powder of pumice stone to preserve the brilliancy of the blades. Bronzes and lacquer work are polished at frequent intervals, and much greater care is

The Tycoon in Seclusion

taken of these ornaments than the most careful housewife in New England bestows upon her "best room." But labor is cheap and time is of little value. You can hire a housemaid for four or five yen a month, which is equivalent to two dollars or two and one-half dollars of our money, so that a dozen Japanese servants can be employed for the same wages that are paid a first-class cook or a butler in the United States.

The servants in a well-ordered household are the most deferential of beings. Every time they bring you a cup of tea or come to remove a dish at dinner or breakfast they will kneel and bow until their foreheads touch the floor. Nor will any of them accept a fee. One night as we were leaving the residence of a Japanese gentleman where we had been taking dinner, one of his servants piloted us through the grounds to the gate where our carriage was waiting, and I attempted to give him a small coin. When I offered it, he clasped his hands together and made a very low bow, keeping his head down until the carriage started.

V
Some Suggestions about Shopping

The shops of Japan are as enticing as those of Paris and the money of the tourist slips away from him faster than he is aware of. Although prices are very low for everything except imported merchandise, one scarcely realizes what inroads he makes on his letter of credit until he comes to figure up how much he is going to need to get home.

The fall of silver has made no difference in the cost of labor or materials, but imported goods are about twice as high as they used to be. For example, one could formerly get an evening suit of the best English diagonal goods for 30 yen, when that sum represented about $25 in gold, but now you have to pay 40 yen or 45, which represents about the same value. There is no difference in the cost of making, but the price of the material has doubled with the depreciation of silver. You can have a first-class English suit made to order for $15 or $18 in gold that would cost you $50 or $60 in the United States. You can buy a pair of trousers for $3 or $4 such as you would pay $10 or $12 for in New York

A DRY-GOODS SHOP.

Some Suggestions about Shopping

or Chicago. The difference is in the low price of labor and the small profit with which the merchants are satisfied. Tailors are paid from 12 to 20 sen a day, which is equivalent to 6 and 10 cents in our money, and if a clothing merchant makes a net profit of 50 or 75 cents on a suit of clothes he is well contented.

The Japanese are good tailors, but the Chinese are better, and, therefore, have the larger portion of the business. There are one or two English tailors in Yokohama, who charge higher prices and are said to be more reliable, but they do not do any better work. The Chinamen are excellent fitters and will make a suit just the way you want it if you will be patient in explaining the details. You can take them an old suit of clothes and they will duplicate it exactly so far as the cut and the fit are concerned.

The same is true of women's clothing. The Chinese and Japanese tailors will make a cloth suit of the best English material for $30 or $40 that would cost $150 in New York and $75 or $80 in London. The prices for all sorts of English clothing are about 30 per cent. less than in London or Paris. If you give a Chinese tailor a London or New York tailor-made dress he will duplicate it as accurately as he does a pair of trousers.

Ordinary underclothing is quite as high as it is in New York, for they are just beginning to

The Yankees of the East

make it in Japan. There is a factory in Tokyo where you can have silk undergarments woven to your measure for about half the London prices. A suit of very light gauze of pure silk costs 8 yen, or $4 gold. A suit of very heavy pure silk will cost 20 yen, or $10. You would pay $12 and $20 for the same things in London. The difference is in the weight of the silk used. They charge you so much a pound for it and so much for the labor of knitting. The same company will make gentlemen's hose of the best Japanese silk for from 50 to 75 cents gold, according to the weight of silk in them. The same quality of ladies' hose costs about twice as much, but the price of everything of this kind depends upon the weight of silk consumed.

When I called at the knitting factory they showed me some underclothes of both silk and wool they were making for the empress. Very few of the ladies of the court wear underclothing of foreign fashion—usually those who have been educated abroad. There are three or four Vassar girls in the circle that surrounds the empress, and several others were educated in the New England colleges for women. While the young men of Japan have been sent to Germany, France, England and Switzerland to study modern life and methods, nearly all of the girls that sought foreign education went to the United States.

Some Suggestions about Shopping

I hope that it is not improper to mention that the underclothes of the Empress of Japan would be called "misses' sizes" by the tradesmen of the United States, for she is a tiny little creature, but her waist is ample and measures thirty-two inches.

Most of the hosiery and underwear knitted in Japan is made in this one shop, with German machinery, operated by women and young girls whose wages average 11 cents a day in our money. This is higher than the ordinary factory operatives receive in Japan. Most of them have to be satisfied with less than 10 cents. At Osaka I saw a great cotton factory filled with women of all ages tending spindles and looms, and showing marvelous dexterity, not one of whom received more than nine cents a day (gold) for twelve hours' work. They begin at six o'clock in the morning and work till six at night, with an intermission of half an hour at nine, twelve and three o'clock. And the wages of the superintendent of the mill were only twenty dollars a month, the same salary that is paid the pastor of the native Presbyterian church in that city.

The wages of seamstresses are even lower, and it seems almost wicked to accept the work they are so poorly paid for. I had a silk kimono made in Kyoto, a garment like the toga of a Roman senator or the gown of a justice of the

The Yankees of the East

supreme court, which all Japanese wear. The silk cost three dollars and forty cents gold, and the merchant charged me fifteen sen or seven and a half cents for the making. I suppose it was an all day's job for some seamstress, and the merchant must have added a commission for himself, or a "squeeze," as they appropriately call it here.

The women who make the beautiful embroideries that are exported from Japan and the men who paint the crêpe goods so artistically receive no higher pay. They work twelve hours a day year after year with a skill and a taste surpassed by no people on earth except the Chinese, perhaps, and their pay does not equal the amount that my lady in England and America spends for the comfort of her lapdog.

I was looking around one day for an artist to paint me a picture of Diabutsu, the impressive bronze idol of Buddha that rears its head above the forest trees down on the southern coast, and asked an art dealer what I ought to pay for a watercolor about thirty-six by twenty-four inches in size.

"Don't let them gouge you out of more than five yen" (two and a half dollars), he replied.

"But I want a good picture."

"The best native artist in Japan would be glad to paint it for that money," was his answer.

The embroideries of Japan are the most at-

Some Suggestions about Shopping

tractive things in the shops, although the silks are alluring. The delicate shades of color and the exquisite designs that are most popular in the local trade are seldom shipped to foreign markets, because the artists and weavers are conservative and stubborn and will not make them of a width suitable for modern dress goods. The silks used in making the beautiful kimonos and obis worn by the women—like those you see in Japanese pictures—are narrow, often less than twelve inches wide, and the most artistic and skillful weavers will not change their looms or their habits. Therefore the best silk fabrics of Japan are not shipped abroad. But by using a little moral suasion and paying a little more you can have any one of these designs reproduced of a width and length to suit you.

The obis—the sashes which the women wear—are the most beautiful fabrics woven in Japan. A Japanese belle regards her obi as an American woman does her diamonds, and although her wardrobe costs very little compared with that of her sister across the sea, two-thirds of its value will be invested in her obi. These precious brocades absorb the most artistic patterns that the designers of Japan produce. They are as thick as leather and as soft as crêpe. It is amazing how the weavers can produce a combination of gold thread and silks that glistens like metal but is as pliable as gauze. The obi usually comes

The Yankees of the East

four yards and a half long and nine inches wide, and you can buy them at any price between $3 and $300. It is said that some of those in the wardrobes of the women of the upper cult in the old feudal times carried as much as $500 worth of pure gold in their threads.

The rarest and most beautiful obis are now obtained of dealers in second-hand goods and in the curio shops, where they have drifted from the kuras (fire-proof wardrobes) of the aristocracy and the geishas (dancing girls) who have become impoverished. The best places to buy them are the cities of the interior. The same is true of all old brocades and embroideries. You pay three times as much for similar articles in Yokohama where foreign buyers are numerous and put up prices, as in Kyoto or in Nagoya, and ten times as much in London or New York. The obi is useless, however, except as an ornament. Its colors are too gay for modern taste, and it is too short and narrow.

The price of embroideries in Japan has increased rapidly with the number of tourists, and those portions of the country which lie within the beaten track of travel are pretty well stripped of fine examples. The art dealers have the best that are left and charge fancy prices for them. But if you can make the acquaintance of a missionary who is in the habit of visiting the towns of the interior, or a tea or silk buyer, he

THE GREAT CASTLE AT NAGOYA.

Some Suggestions about Shopping

will take you to places where gems of art embroidery may be found at prices that are almost incredible. Curtains such as were used centuries ago in the palaces of the daimyos or in the Shinto and Buddhist temples, masses of silk and gold as thick as an Axminster carpet and large enough for a portière or a bedspread, which represent years of labor and the most artistic skill, can be bought for 50 or 60 yen, or half that value in our money. Friezes of the choicest brocades, heavy with gold and silken figures, two feet wide and twenty feet long, representing in their designs historical and mythological scenes, can be had for 25 or 30 yen; and smaller pieces, such as will answer for upholstering chairs or for tablespreads, or sofa pillows, you can buy for $2 or $3 each. When such things get to New York they cost a great deal of money, and the wonder is why some enterprising merchant does not invade the interior of Japan and pick up a large stock of them.

The figures you see on Japanese embroideries and other works of art are:

1. The kirin, which represents the noblest form of animal creation. It is an emblem of perfect good, and holds as prominent a place in the religion and arts of China and Korea as in Japan. It has the body of a deer, the tail of an ox and a single horn. It lives a thousand years, and is a messenger of mercy and good fortune.

The Yankees of the East

2. The feng-hwang, or ho-wo, or phœnix, is the emblem of virtue in the household and government, and the incarnation of the spirits that control and influence good behavior. It has the head of a pheasant, the beak of a swallow and the tail of a bird-of-paradise. Its feathers are of the most gorgeous plumage, representing the five colors, which are emblematic of the cardinal virtues—honesty, obedience, justice, fidelity and benevolence.

3. The kwei or tortoise is the emblem of longevity, the god of the waters. It has the power of transformation and can turn itself into any other kind of beast or fish. It regulates the weather.

4. The lumg or dragon also has the power of transformation, can make itself visible or invisible at will, can reduce itself to the size of a silk worm or swell out large enough to fill the whole earth. It is the embodiment of force; guards the gates of heaven and can give or withhold prosperity.

5. The mitsu tomoye is a sort of monogram, in a circle, usually in three colors, and is found at the end of all the tiles and ridgepoles on the housetops of Japan, upon lanterns, the heads of all the drums, the signs of business houses, and is commonly used in all forms of decoration in temples, palaces, shops and homes. The three segments which curl up together to com-

Some Suggestions about Shopping

pose the circle have a deep philosophical meaning, and represent the trinity of elements—earth, water and air—which combined to form the origin of matter and are necessary for the existence of mankind. It is introduced in the crests of no less than eight of the ancient princes, and appears upon the flag of Korea.

6. The manji is the Buddhist cross, which was brought from India 2,000 years ago, but it appears in the frescoes of the pyramids of Egypt, in the palaces of Pompeii, in the catacombs of Rome, in the Etruscan tombs, in the arts of ancient Greece, in the religious embroideries and missals of mediæval Europe, in old English heraldry, and is known in Norway as Thor's hammer. You find it everywhere in Buddhist temples, as common as the cross in Christian art and architecture, and its name "manji" is a Chinese term that signifies "ten thousand;" probably because it is a talisman against that number of evil spirits. You find it everywhere, quite as common as the mitsu tomoye, on armor, weapons, fans, flags, lanterns, banners and crests.

7. The cock is the emblem of peace, and the tiger of war. There is a drum shaped like a barrel at the entrance of every temple, which people beat to attract the attention of the gods, and that appears frequently in decorative art.

Besides these there is a whole menagerie of

The Yankees of the East

mythical monsters in the demonology of Japan which are drawn upon for decorative purposes.

The peony is the sign of perfection. The sixteen-petal chrysanthemum is the crest of the emperor, and cannot be used by his subjects except upon articles intended for him or for official purposes.

A kami is any kind of a god or supernatural power, supposed to abide in forests; and the people hang votive offerings to them upon the limbs of trees, writing prayers and poems of praise upon pieces of paper and twisting them about the twigs. They are the especial patrons of the agricultural classes. Farmers worship them in the seasons of planting and harvesting so as to secure favorable results, and women make offerings to secure their good-will before undertaking any kind of household employment. There are little shrines dedicated to their honor along all the highways of Japan and the common people never pass them without offering a prayer.

The Japanese are great methodists — they follow forms. If they have precedents or experience of their own or other people that apply to matters of present importance they are all right, but if a new point comes up they are not equal to it and are puzzled as to the proper course to pursue. They have small power of originality and analysis. Their memory has

Some Suggestions about Shopping

been abnormally developed at the sacrifice of the reasoning power. For ages they have studied the proverbs of the sages and apply them to every incident of life until the practice has become hereditary.

They habitually accept facts as facts without inquiring into the causes or the consequences, or, as Mr. Masujima, one of the greatest lawyers of the country, once told his students, "You are always asking what, and not why!" To accept whatever exists and believe that whatever is, is right, is the national tendency, without inquiry into the reasons. It is the result of the teachings of their religion.

If a Japanese meets misfortune or death he submits without a murmur. "Shi-kata-ga-nai" is the word, which means literally, "It can't be helped," and is equivalent to the old proverb that teaches that there is no use crying over spilled milk.

This fatalism permeates every profession and every branch of society, from the coolie to the emperor, and is the heritage of 2,500 years. But it is being gradually modified by the study of mathematics and philosophy and the adoption of foreign customs and ideas.

The Japanese shops are uninviting from the exterior. They have no show-windows; no counters. Their exteriors are blank walls and the entrances are hidden by heavy curtains of

The Yankees of the East

black or dark-blue cloth, bearing large red or white letters in Japanese, which take the place of signboards. Two or three feet from the sidewalk is a raised platform from fifteen or eighteen inches high, and around it a curious assortment of wooden clogs and sandals, for a native customer always leaves her shoes outside when she enters a shop. And when she is buying or looking at goods she sits on the edge of this platform or squats ungracefully on the matting within.

Foreign buyers are allowed to enter with their shoes on and three or four chairs are usually kept for their accommodation. The goods are not spread out on shelves or in showcases, but are kept in boxes and chests usually wrapped in yellow cloth. You take your seat in a chair, a small boy brings you a cup of tea, and you tell the merchant what you want, while he bows himself almost double several times to express his appreciation of your patronage. He shouts his orders to a dozen youngsters in what seems outlandish jargon, but they understand it and come rushing in from some back room or "go down" — which is the word for warehouse — with baskets and boxes full of rolls of the most dainty fabrics. There is usually some one about who speaks a little English and he is sent for. The merchant sits down on the floor, unrolls the goods and chatters away, while his chief clerk

Some Suggestions about Shopping

pretends to explain to you what he is saying. If he cannot show exactly what you want he will ask the honor of sending it to your hotel and the interpreter will usually bring it the next day. There is no limit to the politeness and deference shown by the Japanese tradesman, and he expresses the highest degree of respect for you when he sucks his teeth with a hissing sound.

Prices were never so low as they are in Japan at present, owing to the depreciation of silver, and one may buy nearly all the products of the country, including silks, ceramics and works of art, for just about half of what they cost four or five years ago. This remark, however, does not apply to hotel bills and the general incidental expenses of foreign travelers. As silver has gone down hotel bills have gone up in a corresponding proportion — usually a little more rapidly — and everything else a foreigner has to pay for, except the native goods he purchases, has kept them company.

VI

The Foreign Commerce of Japan

The Japanese government issues an admirable series of official reports each year, including commercial statistics, which are given in great detail and presented in an attractive and convenient manner, both in the French and English languages. These reports equal typographically any similar publications in Europe and America, and in fact contain features that might be imitated by the older nations, particularly Great Britain and the United States.

The total foreign commerce of Japan in 1894 amounted to $115,414,020 in American gold, counting the yen as fifty cents. Of this, $27,798,240 was handled by Japanese merchants, the balance by foreigners residing in the country.

The total exports were $56,623,043, of which $5,225,489 were shipped by native merchants. The total imports were $58,790,977, of which $17,577,750 were brought into the country by natives. It will be seen that the native merchants are much more given to the importation of foreign merchandise than to the shipment of

The Foreign Commerce of Japan

their own products. In 1894 the balance of trade against Japan was $2,117,934, which was due largely to the increased importations of munitions of war. During the same year the imports of silver were 26,227,686 Mexican dollars, and 9,000,000 came from the United States.

The following table shows the total value of merchandise exported to and imported from Europe and the United States during the ten years from 1885 to 1894, inclusive, the values being given in Japanese money:

Country.	Exported From Japan. Yen.	Imported by Japan. Yen.
Great Britain	52,641,903.92	236,415,892.72
France	134,395,116.14	30,414,679.12
Germany	11,654,290.63	51,732,417.08
Austria	2,833,242.60	217,314.67
Belgium	633,601.97	7,440,052.41
Denmark	5,586.50	456,034.70
Holland	910,324.46	430,107.92
Italy	9,054,558.64	1,109,359.95
Portugal	3,073.10	45,340.58
Russia	3,268,314.24	5,573,067.72
Spain	87,612.84	272,751.82
Norway and Sweden	6,287.42	109,530.51
Turkey	95,101.90	25,225.00
Switzerland	2,156,190.33	4,624,127.41
Total trade with Europe	217,745,204.69	338,866,001.61
Total with the United States	264,417,237.97	57,960,908.99
Grand total	482,162,442.66	396,826,910.60

A comparison of the trade of Japan with the United States and Great Britain is even more startling. The following are the totals for the last ten years:

The Yankees of the East

	Exported From Japan. Yen.	Imported by Japan. Yen.
Great Britain	52,641,903.92	236,415,892.72
United States	264,417,237.97	57,960,908.99

Thus in ten years Japan has sold the United States more of her products by 46,672,033 yen than all the nations of Europe combined, and at the same time she has purchased from them more than 281,000,000 yen in excess of her imports from the United States. In other words she has been dependent upon us for a market for her staples, which are silk and tea, and ought to have been a liberal buyer of our merchandise. We have the friendship of the government and the people. Great Britain has their hostility and their trade.

As will be observed in the explanations given by merchants of experience in other chapters of this volume, we are more to blame for this commercial phenomenon than the Japanese themselves. If our merchants and manufacturers had shown the same energy and patience that the British merchants have shown in seeking the trade of Japan, the balance might have been on the other side of the ledger. But the rule in that country is the same as in every other part of the world. If you want to sell goods you must seek the market. The mountain does not go to Mahomet in trade. The conditions in Japan are precisely like those in China, South America, Mexico and the West Indies. The

The Foreign Commerce of Japan

manufacturers of Great Britain, Germany and France, particularly those of the first named country, went to the treaty ports, Yokohoma, Kobe, Nagasaki and other places, as soon as we opened Japan to foreign trade, and camped on the ground. They established agencies, built warehouses, founded banks and took possession of the markets. They found out what goods were wanted, studied the peculiarities and requirements of the people, and furnished what they needed in such a form and style as suited their taste. A few Frenchmen and Germans followed, and representatives of other nationalities in smaller numbers. The manufacturers of America took no interest in the great market that was being developed on the rich little island, because they had so much to do at home. It was no lack of enterprise, nor is it a reflection upon the ability of our people that we have little foreign trade. The home market has been sufficient to absorb all our attention, but now, when our power of production has been multiplied by the development of our industries and the introduction of labor-saving machinery, and we need customers to take our surplus off our hands, we find the markets of Japan, like those of China and the Latin American countries, occupied and controlled by our commercial rivals, and we have got to fight for the plums that fell into their laps.

The Yankees of the East

At the same time these very merchants have been shipping the products of Japan to us because our people are willing to pay better prices for the luxuries of life than those of any other nation.

The following table shows the growth of the foreign trade of Japan during the last ten years:

	EXPORTS.	IMPORTS.
1885	$18,573,345	$19,678,488
1887	26,204,330	22,152,125
1890	28,301,753	40,864,240
1892	45,551,326	35,663,039
1894	56,623,043	58,790,977

The following table shows the distribution of the exports of Japan among the several nations, arranged according to the magnitude of the trade in the year 1894:

	1894.	1892.	1890.
United States	$21,661,778	$19,337,481	$9,901,768
France	9,799,388	9,046,847	4,177,197
Hongkong	8,049,740	6,644,270	4,683,203
China	4,401,896	3,179,429	2,613,747
Great Britain	2,975,098	2,960,976	2,319,490
British India	1,844,024	711,144	296,392
Germany	758,774	470,391	423,461

The remainder of the exports of Japan are sent in small amounts to nearly every nation in the world, mostly tea, rice, silk and curios.

The following table shows the sources from which the imports of Japan come, arranged according to the magnitude of the trade in 1894:

	1894.	1892.	1890.
Great Britain	$21,094,936	$10,394,666	$13,309,552
China	8,750,753	6,254,705	4,424,882
United States	5,491,279	2,994,026	3,437,225
British India	5,280,224	3,832,001	4,455,001
Hongkong	4,499,859	3,492,761	2,747,456
Germany	3,059,271	3,187,524	3,428,479
France	2,174,023	1,810,250	1,934,665

The Foreign Commerce of Japan

It will be noticed that the United States has continued to take a very large portion of the exports of Japan, but has furnished a very small portion of the imports of that country, while Great Britain enjoys a trade that is exactly the reverse. In other words, in 1894 we sold Japan $5,491,279 worth of goods and bought $21,661,788 of her products, while Great Britain sold her $21,094,936 worth of merchandise, and bought only $2,319,490 of her products. That is not a question of distance, for San Francisco is only 4,750 miles from Japan, while the nearest British port is 11,600 miles.

It will be seen, too, that the growth of our export trade to Japan has been comparatively slow, the increase having been but $2,054,054 during the last four years, while the exports from England to Japan during that period have jumped $7,685,384. In the same time our imports from Japan have increased $11,760,010, while England purchased last year only $655,608 more than she did four years ago.

France suffers quite as much as we do in the matter of trade. Like the United States she takes the raw silk and tea of the Japanese, while England buys little and sells them all sorts of things. Much of the trade that is credited to Hongkong goes to Great Britain, being transhipped at that city. Great Britain gets her tea from China and Formosa, while we use more from Japan.

The Yankees of the East

The native merchants carry on a larger trade with Asia than with any other continent, leaving the foreign merchants to deal with the United States and the European nations. Their business last year with British India amounted to $4,000,000; with China $3,750,000; with Korea $2,500,000, and with Hongkong $1,500,000. Their trade with Great Britain last year amounted to $7,878,500, and with the United States $5,219,000. It is a singular fact, too, that a large proportion of the foreign trade carried on by native merchants is the importation of manufactured merchandise. Of their trade with Asia $7,500,000 was imports and $4,250,000 exports; of their trade with England $8,500,000 was imports and only $1,000,000 exports, while of their trade with the United States $1,315,000 was imports and $4,008,000 exports. The chief exports from Japan in 1894 were as follows:

Raw silk	$21,446,375
Textile fabrics, mostly silks	8,867,743
Food products, mostly rice	5,416,098
Tea	3,965,243
Coal	3,298,214
Metals, mostly copper	3,015,180
Matches	1,897,817
Drugs and medicines	1,230,811
Floor matting	987,746
Porcelains	742,426
Fish oil and vegetable wax	639,095
Laquer ware	398,769
Umbrellas	388,031
Straw plaiting	371,699
Bamboo and wooden ware	289,498
Tobacco	274,137
Fans	171,533
Paper and stationery	163,320

The Foreign Commerce of Japan

It is a curious fact that 10,277,401 fans were shipped from Japan that year, 2,348,810 umbrellas, 134,209 screens, 455,659 paper lanterns, 13,843,022 gross of matches and 66,223 lily bulbs.

The exports of silk were larger than ever before, although it is scarcely fair to compare the figures with 1893, as that was a poor year all around. There has recently been a very large increase in the exportation of piece goods, and especially cotton, since modern machinery was introduced and cotton factories erected. In 1892 the number of pieces of cotton goods exported was 623,039. In 1894 the total was 1,894,928, In 1892 the export of cotton yarn were valued at $3,859; in 1894 $477,764. Japan is now exporting gloves, hats and caps, boots and shoes, stockings and fabrics of both wool and cotton goods of every variety.

Camphor is the largest item among the drugs, and was shipped to England and the United States, but I find $143,070 worth of menthol crystals and $242,769 worth of peppermint oil.

Of food products Japan exports wheat, barley, beans, peas, flour, fish, mushrooms, potatoes, rye and salt, and the records show $581,227 worth of cuttlefish, $313,575 of edible sea-weed and $51,107 worth of sharks' fins. These went to China. Beer is sent to the Asiatic countries near by and the Phillippine islands; tobacco to

The Yankees of the East

China and Korea. France is the largest buyer of bronzes; bamboo furniture is shipped everywhere; coal to China, Hongkong, British India and the Phillippine islands; copper to China, Hongkong, Great Britain and Germany. The United States takes 95 per cent of the hemp and cotton rugs which have recently come into fashion, and the demand has increased so much that the value of $80,000, which represented the exports in 1892, had been increased to over $600,000 in 1894.

The increased manufacture of cotton goods in Japan is beginning to have an effect on the British market, for her exports are already considerable and are increasing at the rate of several hundred per cent each year. And, sooner or later, the cotton manufacturers of the United States will feel the competition, because the large proportion of the exports are piece goods. British India, China and Hongkong are the largest buyers, but a considerable amount goes to the Hawaiian islands, Korea, Australia and eastern Russia. The exports of cotton yarn to China were valued at more than $400,000. One hundred thousand suits of cotton underclothes were sent to India, China and Hongkong, for Japan is not only making her own knit goods now, but is soon going to assist the United States and European countries in furnishing the world's supply.

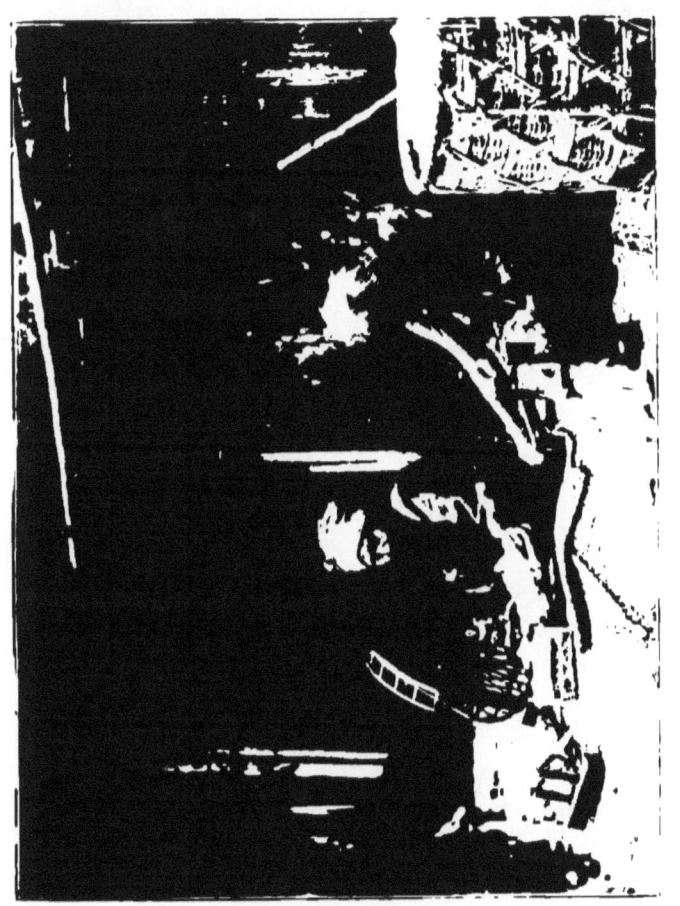

THE OLD-FASHIONED WAY OF SPINNING.

The Foreign Commerce of Japan

We are the largest buyers of fans, taking 2,152,243; England next, then Italy, France, China, Germany, Spain, British India and Austria, in the order named. Considerable flour was sent to Siberia and Korea; the furs went to England, the glass and iron ware to China and Korea, and it is curious to note that the Japanese jinrikisha is being introduced into the neighboring countries, probably for the accommodation of foreigners. India took 1,950 of these admirable vehicles in 1894, Hongkong 947, China 38 and other countries 72.

Like the bamboo, the famous lacquered ware of Japan is sent everywhere, Great Britain, France, Germany, India, Hongkong, Australia, Holland and the United States being the largest buyers. Nearly fourteen million gross of matches are shipped abroad annually, the greater part going to Hongkong, China and British India.

The United States takes ninety-five per cent of the floor matting exported and nearly half the stationery. Considerable wall paper is sent to Great Britain and the United States. Fancy goods made of paper go everywhere, and screens are furnished to nearly all of the nations of the earth.

Crystal menthol goes to Germany, France, Great Britain and the United States, mushrooms to Hongkong and China. Germany takes half the peppermint oil. The remainder is divided

The Yankees of the East

between England, France and the United States. We are the largest buyers of porcelains, taking about one-third of the whole; Hongkong, Great Britain, France and India the remainder. Salt, wheat and saké (the native brandy) are sent to Korea and Siberia. Most of the plaited straw goes to Great Britain and the United States, and the umbrellas and toilet soap to China, Hongkong and India.

The United States is the largest buyer of raw silk, taking nearly one-half of the whole product. There has been a considerable increase of late in the shipments to France, which is the second buyer. Italy and Switzerland also are taking raw silk from Japan. The United States takes almost two-thirds of the silk piece goods. France comes second; those two countries buy seven-eighths of all that is exported. Great Britain bought less than $250,000 in 1894, and that was a very large increase over 1892, when she bought only $39,000 worth.

The shipments of silk handkerchiefs in 1894 amounted to 1,435,674 dozen, of which the United States took 834,746 dozen, Great Britain 177,248 dozen, and France 139,337 dozen. The rest were sent to the four corners of the world.

The exports of tea amounted to 37,390,822 catty, a catty being one and one-third pounds. One hundred catty make a picul—133 pounds. The United States takes three-fourths of the tea

The Foreign Commerce of Japan

produced in Japan. British America is the second buyer.

The following table shows the general character of the merchandise imported into Japan and the value of each class of goods included in her imports during the year 1894, the amount having been reduced to American gold:

Raw cotton,	$9,551,961
Machinery,	7,974,542
Sugar,	6,662,260
Breadstuffs, including rice,	5,877,068
Cotton yarn,	4,888,682
Iron and steel,	4,589,384
Woolen goods,	3,991,440
Cotton fabrics,	2,888,266
Oil and wax, mostly kerosene,	2,845,996
Drugs and medicines,	1,798,140
Dyes and paints,	986,641
Furs, hides and leather,	904,034
Provisions,	886,602
Copper, brass and lead,	876,973
Books and stationery,	451,782
Oil cakes,	411,097
Hemp and jute,	403,961
Other textiles,	279,357
Silk goods,	261,492
Wines and liquors,	251,672
Glassware,	183,883
Clothing,	179,811

As will be noticed, raw cotton is the largest item of import and it furnishes an illustration of the very rapid increase in the manufacture of textiles in Japan. The imports of cotton have doubled within the last two years, but only $1,340,000 was sent direct from the United States. The balance was bought through commission houses at Liverpool and trans-shipped at that port.

The Yankees of the East

Great Britain furnished ninety-nine per cent of the cotton yarns and threads and nearly all the textiles that were imported. They consisted of cotton drills, shirtings, sheetings, lawns, prints, satins, handkerchiefs and velvets. The second item of importance, machinery, covers a very large variety of articles, as follows: Electric plants, locomotive engines ($790,000), mining machinery, spinning machinery ($1,429,000), boilers and engines ($107,000). Most of it was furnished by Great Britain.

The sugar that Japan imports comes originally from Formosa, but is refined in Hongkong, but there is going to be a decided change in this business. Now that Formosa has been annexed to Japan, the raw sugar will be shipped direct and refined there. It is the intention of the government to develop the sugar industry in Formosa, which, although extensive, is conducted in a very primitive manner. That island is similar in latitude, climate, soil and resources to Cuba, and is likely to give as much trouble in government for several years as Cuba has given Spain.

Although Japan exported nearly $5,500,000 worth of rice in 1894, she imported nearly as much, which came from Siam, French India, China, Korea, and British India. The reason for this freak of trade is that the people ship their own product to Europe, where it brings the

The Foreign Commerce of Japan

highest prices, and import a cheaper grade from China and Korea. The Japanese rice is said to be the best in the world, and to have a particular flavor that is more agreeable to Europeans. Other breadstuffs imported into the country are beans, peas, and millet, which come mostly from China and Korea, and about $306,000 worth of flour from the United States.

England furnishes the greater portion of the iron and steel imported into Japan. The principal items under this head in 1894 were: rails ($604,000), bar and rod ($669,000), iron nails ($666,000), which came mostly from Germany, pig iron ($376,000), plate and sheet ($450,000), pipes and tubes ($242,000), wire ($42,000), galvanized sheets ($78,000), and a little telegraph and steel wire.

The woolen imports consisted of raw wool from Australia, yarns from Germany, cloths from Germany and England, flannels from Germany, and blankets from Great Britain.

It has often been said by facetious travellers that the only exports from the United States to Japan are kerosene oil and missionaries. As a matter of fact the former article furnishes the largest item in our commerce, averaging 36,000,000 gallons, valued at $2,039,000, while Russia sent 9,500,000, gallons valued at $526,000.

The drugs and medicines used in Japan come mostly from Great Britain, the dyes from Ger-

The Yankees of the East

many, and the perfumeries and cosmetics from France. We furnish a good deal of leather, but most of the hides come from India and Korea.

A good deal of condensed milk is shipped into Japan from the United States and Switzerland, as they have very few cows there. The butter comes from the United States, Holland and Denmark in tins. The grass of the country is not suitable for dairy food. Alfalfa has been successfully grown, but you see very little of it. Americans who keep cows import hay from the United States. Other provisions come from Great Britain and the United States in the form of preserved fish, fruits, meats and vegetables.

Very little wine and liquor is imported into Japan, and that is used almost exclusively by foreigners. There are several breweries and distilleries in the country and some wine is made, but the national drink is saké—a brandy made from rice, which is used extensively by all classes, but you see very little intoxication.

The annual returns of the foreign trade of Japan for 1894, show a list of 196 articles imported from the United States, 204 from France, 279 from Germany, and 335 from Great Britain.

The list of the United States contains nearly everything that can come under the head of

The Foreign Commerce of Japan

general merchandise, from lead pencils to locomotives, but, as I have said, the chief value is in petroleum. The exports from Germany, France, and England are nearly all manufactured goods, and consists of articles that might be furnished by the United States at equally low prices. Aside from machinery the largest part of the imports of Japan are raw materials for their own factories to work over into articles of merchandise, many of which are sent abroad.

A result of the remarkable national spirit that was aroused in Japan by the late war, is a determination on the part of the native merchants to control both the import and export trade. The foreign commerce of Japan has always been conducted very largely by foreign commission houses in the treaty ports, which have stood as middlemen between the producer, the manufacturer and the merchant of Japan, and those in foreign countries who have bought from or sold goods to him; but now the natives are determined to abolish this system and trade direct. This movement is not so much to avoid the commissions charged by the middlemen, as to gratify the national pride. The following tables, from official sources, show the comparative volume of trade handled by the foreign and the native merchants during the last ten years:

The Yankees of the East

Year.	Exports through Japanese. yen.	Exports through Foreigners. yen.
1885	2,303,743	31,390,019
1886	5,713,201	41,628,570
1887	6,555,436	43,996,087
1888	7,142,916	56,599,289
1889	6,900,775	61,641,543
1890	6,207,489	48,767,636
1891	8,839,025	69,144,862
1892	11,471,009	77,943,924
1893	14,362,029	74,485,809
1894	20,348,535	92,897,551

Year.	Imports through Japanese. yen.	Imports through Foreigners. yen.
1885	2,344,986	25,724,772
1886	2,566,150	28,332,800
1887	5,030,231	37,365,703
1888	8,593,755	53,820,247
1889	9,778,014	54,349,248
1890	19,629,759	61,033,110
1891	14,324,841	47,692,803
1892	13,932,769	56,263,748
1893	16,891,696	70,908,139
1894	34,324,804	53,157,151

This shows a steady increase in the articles exported and imported through Japanese firms, the exports having increased more than six times, and the imports more than fourteen times during the past decade. But it was only a natural increase accompanying the general expansion of trade, that which passed through the hands of foreign firms having increased in the same proportion. The fact that Japan's foreign trade is in the hands of foreigners remains unchanged.

The Tokyo chamber of commerce recently memorialized parliament on this subject, asking

The Foreign Commerce of Japan

the assistance of the government in securing the control of foreign trade. They even went so far as to demand the establishment of native steamship lines, in order that they might not be dependent upon foreigners for transportation facilities; and the native merchants and manufacturers have just organized what is known as the " Foreign Trade Association," whose object may be inferred from the following list of committees:

1. To report facts important to exporters.
2. To secure increased facilities.
3. To prevent the exportation of spurious products.
4. To secure government encouragement for the export trade.
5. For the education of able men for the export trade.
6. To encourage intimacy between producers and exporters.
7. To encourage the development of industries for export.
8. To examine the commercial conditions and requirements of foreign markets.

There is the utmost friendliness towards the United States among all classes, from the emperor to the coolie, and it is exhibited on all occasions. There is scarcely a merchant in all Japan, except those who have been educated in England, that would not prefer to trade with the

The Yankees of the East

United States, and the government has repeatedly shown its good will by offering to pay higher prices for supplies from America than the same articles would cost in Europe. Our government could make any sort of alliance, political or commercial, with Japan. A member of the ministry remarked to me:

"I can conceive of no calamity more painful than a misunderstanding between our countries."

The fourth of July is always a great day in Yokohama. All the subjects of European nations residing there, all the Japanese officials, high and low, and all strangers who happen to be within those gates, always join with the American colony in celebrating the anniversary of our independence. The United States minister and consul-general hold receptions in the morning, and in the afternoon there is usually a dancing party and luncheon upon a man-of-war in the harbor. The Grand hotel, which is the center of social life in Japan, is crowded with gaily dressed parties, and in the evening fireworks and set pieces are displayed from a float anchored in the bay.

Last year the celebration was attended with more enthusiasm than ever before, and from daylight to midnight the air was filled with the odor of powder and explosions, music, rockets and red fire. The flagship Baltimore, in command of Admiral Carpenter, came up from the

The Foreign Commerce of Japan

China sea to do the honors, and the reception given by the officers during the afternoon was one of the most elegant and enjoyable affairs ever known in Japan. The ships in the harbor were all gayly dressed with bunting, and as there were ten men-of-war and eighteen merchant ships at anchor, they made quite a spectacle. The British flagship Centurion, of 10,500 tons, and one of the most formidable of her majesty's navy, was attended by the cruisers Edgar, Undaunted, Leander and Alacrity. The French flagship Bayard, the German cruiser Itlis and the Russian cruisers Mandjur and Razbonyk made especial demonstrations, and nearly everybody you met on the street had a cravat or a handkerchief made to resemble the American flag, or a bit of red, white and blue ribbon tied in his buttonhole.

And the pleasantest part of it was that the enthusiasm seemed to be universal. There is sharp competition in trade between our people and the Europeans, but not so much as between themselves, and we are the next friend to each of them, so that all joined with the most cordial feeling in the celebration of our birthday. The four British dailies suspended publication, most of the business houses and all the banks, even those owned and managed by Englishmen, closed for the day, and no city in America observed the occasion more generally. Nor is any

The Yankees of the East

foreign holiday more universally observed in Japan. The birthday of Queen Victoria and the anniversary of her coronation are made much of wherever Englishmen are found, and the French and Germans also have their national fêtes, but their celebrations are limited to the subjects of their own nation and are not general like the Fourth of July. Nor do the officials and people of Japan take part in any other holiday. They always observe the Fourth of July with as much ardor as one of their own great days, but entirely overlook similar anniversaries of other nations.

Americans are more patriotic when they are abroad than when they are at home. The stars and stripes are always more beautiful when you see them flying in a foreign harbor, and you sing "Home, Sweet Home" with a great deal more fervor when you are bouncing around in half a gale of wind at sea.

The government of the United States is especially fortunate in the character of its representatives in Japan, and the American colony is composed of a high class of people. Mr. Dun of Ohio, our minister; Mr. Herrod of Indiana, the secretary of legation; Commander Barber, the naval attaché; Mr. McIvor of Iowa, the consul-general; Mr. McLean, the vice-consul-general; Mr. Skidmore, the deputy consul-general, and Dr. Abercrombie, the consul at Naga-

The Foreign Commerce of Japan

saki, are all gentlemen of the highest character and universally popular. I did not hear a single complaint or criticism of any one of them while I was in Japan, and that is quite remarkable, because visiting and resident Americans in other parts of the world have an irresistible tendency to say disagreeable things about the diplomatic and consular agents of their government.

There are three commercial exchanges in Tokyo, at which business is conducted upon the same general principles as at the board of trade in Chicago, the New York stock exchange and other similar institutions, except that a larger proportion of the trades are for actual delivery and a smaller proportion for speculative profit. At the stock exchange government bonds, railway bonds and shares and other securities are dealt in, and the organization dates back twenty years. Another exchange, at which nothing but rice is dealt in, is even older, and was started in 1870 soon after the restoration. The third is a sort of miscellaneous affair, at which all staple products except rice is bought and sold, including wheat, flour, corn, barley, oats, beans, salt, sugar, oil, coal, cotton, iron and other metals.

During the last six months of 1895 at the stock exchange $10,300,000 in government bonds were bought and sold, or a daily average of about $71,527, and forty-seven different kinds of stocks

The Yankees of the East

to the value of $60,493,503. The total number of transactions involved was 60,380, or an average of about 410 a day. There are seventy members of the stock exchange, all of them active brokers, who have their offices in little narrow alleys surrounding the old building, which has been used ever since the exchange was organized. They are divided into five groups or companies for the sake of convenience, each being in charge of an experienced member, who is the representative of his group in the executive committee and board of management, and is expected to look out for the good behavior and discipline of the members of his division. There are no arbitrary dividing lines, and a broker may select his own division if he has a choice, but they are generally arranged according to the location of their offices, and are known by the points of the compass. All disputes or appeals from the officials of the board are decided by the heads of division, who, sitting as a committee, are the final authority in all such matters.

More than fifty per cent. of the sales are genuine and for actual investment. The remainder are speculative. There is very small encouragement for speculation, because prices fluctuate but little and bidding is limited to ten sen, or five cents a share. The smallest deal allowed is five shares. Three hundred shares is considered a

The Foreign Commerce of Japan

very large transaction. A sale of five hundred shares creates great excitement, and one thousand, bought or sold, will shake the market. The average transactions are fifty and one hundred shares. The government bonds and most of the railway shares are at a par of fifty yen, instead of one hundred as with us.

The exchange has a rake-off on every transaction, which includes the government tax, and is made plain to everybody by printed placards posted in conspicuous places. On all trades involving ten yen or less, the treasury of the exchange gets seven-tenths of a sen; over ten and less than fifty, seven sen; over fifty and less than seventy-five, eleven sen; over seventy-five and less than one hundred, fifteen sen, and so on up to transactions of five hundred yen which pay the exchange sixty-one sen each. A sen was originally equivalent to our cent, and one hundred sen make one yen, which is equivalent to a Mexican silver dollar.

The exchange is a stock company, in which all of the brokers own shares. A man must own at least one share to enjoy the privileges of the institution, but nearly all his money comes back to him in dividends, and, being limited as well as profitable, shares are in great demand. Last year, which was unusually prosperous on account of the speculative excitement caused by the war, a forty per cent. dividend was declared after pay-

The Yankees of the East

ing all the running expenses and the government tax.

The brokers' commissions are officially arranged in a similar manner. On fifty shares or less they are allowed to charge their customers fifteen sen, which is the lowest; and then the commissions increase with every fifty shares until the charge for a deal of three hundred shares is seventy sen, and four hundred and fifty shares one yen or one dollar. No provision is made for deals of more than five hundred shares, but when they occur commissions are charged in the same proportion.

The exchange is open six days in the week, and is closed on Sunday out of respect to the Christian religion. In summer there are seven calls a day—at 8, 9, 10, 11, 12, 2 and 3 o'clock. In winter the 8 o'clock call is omitted. There is some trading between calls, but that is considered irregular. About five or ten minutes before the hour one of the janitors goes out to the front door and rings a big dinner-bell, which is the signal for business. The brokers then begin flocking in from their offices, bareheaded, barefooted and wearing the native dress, which is a kimono, usually of some dark blue stuff, which is open at the neck and down in front, and secured around the waist by a silk belt. Under this kimono they wear an undershirt of cotton gauze or silk, or some other light material, and

The Foreign Commerce of Japan

perhaps another white cotton kimono next to the skin. But their legs are bare, and in the excitement of trading they throw back their clothing to such an extent that one might imagine that the whole party had just dropped in on their way to the bath in their bathing robes.

When the clock strikes the hour they gather in front of a platform upon which three clerks and an umpire are sitting or standing. The signal for business is given by the chief clerk, who sits in the middle, by clapping together two blocks of woods that are inscribed with Japanese characters. One of the clerks then calls out the names of the different stocks in alphabetical order, hanging up a long board at the same time which contains the same titles. The brokers then begin to clamor and wave their hands in the air in a most excited manner. Those who desire to sell make a motion away from themselves toward the others. Those who desire to buy a make a motion toward their faces with the palm of their hand, at the same time yelling at the top of their voices the price they are willing to give or accept. When they decide to buy or sell, as the case may be, they strike hands three times and the caller on the platform sings out the trade, giving the names of the persons, the number of shares and the price, which are recorded in a peculiar manner by a quick-witted clerk who never looks up from his paper, but

The Yankees of the East

keeps his ink brush moving like an electric current all the time. The umpire, who is an old broker retired from business, stands by to settle disputes, but is very seldom appealed to. I am informed that there has not been a single controversy to be settled by the board so far during the present year.

The brokers keep no account of their own sales or purchases, but leave that all to the clerks of the exchange through whom the business is done. When trading languishes and it appears that nobody wants to buy or sell any more the caller claps his sticks together, which is the signal for closing business in that particular stock, and proceeds with the rest through the list in that order to the end. In dull times the whole forty-seven stocks in the list are gone through with in ten minutes, but often, when there is excitement, they occupy the whole hour, and a new set of clerks come out to relieve those that were on duty.

At the close of the call the clerks retire to their offices, and the record clerk takes his blanks, which are ruled in blue for the afternoon and red for the morning, and reads off to three or four clerks sitting around him the list of transactions, while they separate them according to the different brokers, placing a memorandum for the buyer on one kind of blank of a certain color and that for the seller upon another. The

The Foreign Commerce of Japan

original records look as if a baby had been scratching upon them with a pen and ink. A mark in the left-hand corner, resembling a seal, is the name of the stock; an X is the date. The first column shows the number of shares, the second column the price, the third column the name of the broker buying and the fourth column the broker selling.

When the clerks have finished the records they send a statement, which is a delivery certificate, to the buyer, and a similar document, which is a receipt, to the seller; and the transaction is completed through the office of the board. At the close of the day each broker is furnished with a statement of his transactions during the several calls upon another blank. The exchange as a body becomes responsible for all transactions that are made under its auspices. In other words, it guarantees that the buyer will accept and pay for whatever he purchases, and that the seller will deliver.

Business on the rice exchange is conducted in a similar manner, but usually with a greater degree of excitement, as rice is the great staple of the country. The usual day's transactions are about 30,000 kokus, a koku being equivalent to five English bushels, and worth $8.50 to $9. During the month of June, 1895, 743,440 kokus were bought and sold, of which only a little more than 100,000 were for actual delivery, which

The Yankees of the East

shows a larger amount of speculation than on the stock exchange. A bell is rung before each call; there are seven calls a day in summer and six in winter, and ninety brokers are members of the exchange. A quick-witted clerk makes the same sort of a record, although a simpler one, because there is only one article to be dealt in.

Nobody but the clerk himself can read these hieroglyphics, but he never makes a mistake. He has been engaged in this work for fourteen years and his records have never yet been questioned. This is very remarkable because of the excitement and confusion that always prevail on the board during business hours. The record is somewhat simplified by the fact that every broker has his rubric, or official sign, which is known to the clerks and is used in keeping the records instead of the name of his firm. He uses it as a seal on all his official documents and none are authentic unless they bear it.

Formerly the merchant class were the lowest in the social scale in Japan. They were even below policemen. Soldiers ranked the highest of the middle caste and next to the nobility; then the farmers, artisans and artists, mechanics, and finally the merchants, next above the coolie or laboring class. One of the results of the reformation in Japan has been to partially reverse this order. There also been several other classes

The Foreign Commerce of Japan

introduced into what may be termed the commercial caste—manufacturers, brokers, managers of corporations and scientific and professional men. The social scale is now as follows:

1. Bankers, high officials of corporations, scientific and professional men who are graduates of the university.
2. Brokers, manufactures and wholesale merchants.
3. Retail merchants.
4. Artists and skilled artisans.
5. Soldiers and policemen.
6. Farmers.
7. Laborers or coolies.

The war with China, has, however, elevated the military class in the social scale, but their new position is probably only temporary.

VII
Railways and 'Rikishas

There are no navigable rivers in Japan. There are a few canals of local importance, and one of them, which connects Kyoto, the ancient capital, with a neighboring lake, is a marvel of engineering, as it passes through a chain of rugged mountains and a tunnel several miles long. In former years the traffic of the empire was conducted by means of the canals and a system of highways which were constructed and controlled by the government. The chief of these were the Tokaido, which means "Eastern sea road," running from Kyoto eastward and northward, following the coast line as far as practicable to the city of Yedo, which is called Tokyo now. Another road called the Nakasendo Kaido went northward from Kyoto, bisecting the interior of the empire and following the chain of mountains which furnish a backbone for Japan. A third was the Piku Kaido, which led northward from Tokyo to the extreme provinces. From these roads branches were constructed to the settled portions of the country.

Railways and 'Rikishas

The whole system was admirably planned for the convenience of commerce and travel.

The Tokaido was the main highway, like the royal road of the Incas that follows the breast of the Andes from Ecuador to Chile, and is still one of the wonders of the world. But the Japanese highways were less difficult of construction, because the country is not so mountainous nor so rocky as Peru. The Tokaido is narrow and well paved after a fashion that suggests our macadam pavement. It slopes sharply from the center to the gutters, which have conduits to carry the water into the irrigating ditches and reservoirs on either side for the use of the farmers.

Few vehicles were known in Japan until 1868. Pack horses were used to a considerable extent, but most of the burdens were carried on the backs of men.

For centuries the Tokaido was traversed twice a year by the daimios—the feudal princes of Japan—and their gorgeous retinues, who once a year visited Tokyo to pay their respects to the shogun. Each was accompanied by thousands of knights, called samurai, and coolies, who bore their armor and trappings and the tribute they were required to pay annually at court. At intervals on this, as well as on other great highways, fine tea houses were erected, in which their highnesses found refreshment and sleeping accommodations, and, like the inns of England

The Yankees of the East

in the time of Queen Elizabeth, they were gay resorts for the exchange of gossip and the enjoyment of amusements. The avenue was lined with fine trees and bordered with hedges, many of which still exist. The roadway, which was made of crushed pebbles, was as smooth as a floor and never muddy, for its surface shed the rain like a roof, and during the dry season it was sprinkled with water several times a day.

Most of the travelers went on foot, but the princes and others of high degree were carried in sedan chairs or palanquins, similar to those of India and Turkey, while those of the lower classes who were ill, or able to afford it, rode in kagos—modest chairs of bamboo carried by two coolies. The etiquette of the road was well defined and rigidly enforced. When the trains of two princes met the prince of lesser rank dismounted from his chair and drew his followers up by the roadside to salute his superior as he passed. But these meetings were avoided when possible. There were often collisions between the followers of the princes at the tea houses and along the way, and their two-handed swords did great execution. Time and distance were not considered, but dignity was maintained at any cost.

Since the reformation, however, these highways have been used exclusively for local communication. They are kept in good repair by

Railways and 'Rikishas

the county authorities, and you meet a great many coolies carrying packs of merchandise on their backs from the cities to the country shopkeepers, and hauling carts loaded with produce from the farms to the market; but the greatest use of the roads at present is by the jinrikisha—the little carriage drawn by man power so common in Japan. The roads are well adapted to them, and all the passenger traffic in the interior is carried on in these vehicles. The kagos and the sedan chairs are almost entirely obsolete. You see them only in the museums.

Those who are familiar with the map of Japan will remember that it has a long and narrow territory shaped something like a crescent. It is not more than two hundred miles wide at the widest, and at places it is less than fifty. It is divided throughout its entire length by continuous ranges of high hills and mountains running almost parallel with the coast. Therefore when the Japanese government began its system of public improvements, which are in many cases remarkable, it planned for parallel lines of railway following practically the general direction of the original highways, departing from it only as the topography of the country and the location of commercial and industrial centers required, and tapping occasionally the ocean ports to connect with coasting vessels and steamships from foreign lands.

The Yankees of the East

The railways along the eastern and southern coast, which is the most populous section of the country, are very nearly completed. The western branch of the system is only partially constructed, and much of the traffic of that portion is carried on by sea. The most important section of the railway system was built and is still owned and managed by the government. The remaining lines and the steamship companies belong to private parties, but are liberally subsidized.

The government line connects the two capitals, Tokyo and Kyoto, and has various branches, with a total mileage of 559 miles. There are twenty-two corporations operating private lines, with capital stock varying from 100,000 to 20,000,000 yen, but they are all under government control and are subject to the jurisdiction of the minister of communication, whose regulations are similar to those of the interstate commerce commission in the United States.

The original government roads were experimental. They were commenced in 1870, and with the idea of giving a practical test to the several methods. American, English, French and German engineers were employed to superintend the same style of construction to which they were accustomed in their home countries. The natural result was an excessive expenditure of money, but it was not wasted. The education of native engineers was expensive, but it

Railways and 'Rikishas

was valuable, and the lessons thus learned have made the Japanese the most capable and economical railway engineers in the world.

The first piece of road, between Yokohama and Tokyo, a dead level eighteen miles long, hugging closely the shore of the Bay of Tokyo, cost $200,000, gold, a mile. It is as solid and as well equipped as any line that runs out of London. The Japanese studied every step intently, and they are now constructing their own track at a cost of 18,000 or 20,000 yen, or $9,000 and $10,000 a mile, over much more difficult country.

After a fair test the English system was adopted as the most suitable and best adapted to the requirements of the people, who are very thickly settled and travel a great deal, but only for short distances. There are still a few foreigners left in the railway service—perhaps half a dozen or so—but the government is getting rid of them and substituting natives. And up to within a short time all the construction material and rolling stock was imported from England and Germany, but American locomotives have been found more useful on the heavy grades and are being substituted. It will not be long, however, before the Japanese will be making all their own rolling stock. They are already building freight and passenger cars, and have built several locomotives in their shops,

The Yankees of the East

buying certain parts in England and making the simpler portions there. The work is still in the experimental stage. Steel and iron are so cheap in Europe that they find it more economical to buy than to make what they want, particularly as their ore is not of a good quality.

The government railways in Japan are well and economically managed, which is not the usual rule in other countries. The receipts from passenger traffic constituted 78.4 per cent of the whole last year, from freight 19.1 per cent, and from miscellaneous sources 2.5 per cent. The small earnings from freight is due to the fact that nearly all the roads meet with active competition from coasting vessels, while in the interior the "short hauls" are still monopolized by coolies, who carry packs on their backs or haul heavily loaded carts with the aid of a cow or an ox. Horses are very seldom seen except in the foreign settlements. You can ride for days through the country without seeing a single horse, either in the villages or on the farms. I was told by good authority that there are only 300,000 horses in Japan, with a population of over 40,000,000, and that a large per cent of those belong to the army and other branches of the government.

The railway from Tokyo, the new capital of the empire, to Aomori, at the northern extremity of the main island, runs parallel with the Pacific

Railways and 'Rikishas

coast, from fifty to sixty miles distant. It is 450 miles in length.

The government road from Tokyo westward to Kyoto and Kobe, hugs the coast a distance of 376 miles, and passes through some of the most important towns in the empire—Yokohama, Kodzu, Nagoya, and Osaka. This road has been extended westward by private parties along the northern coast of the Inland sea to Hiroshima, a distance of 189 miles, and it is proposed to continue it to Nagasaki, the principal port on the west coast, which is only a short distance across the Yellow sea from Tien-Tsin and Shanghai. It also runs to Yobuko, at the top of the northernmost peninsula of the western coast, which is only a short distance across the Korean strait from Fusan, the southern port of Korea.

The western section of this road extends from Moji along the northern coast and then southward along the western coast 180 miles to Kumamoto. The distance yet to be constructed to connect the extreme northern and eastern cities of Japan with its extreme western and southern parts is 156 miles, for which surveys have been made. Through traffic is now provided by means of a line of small steamers between Hiroshima and Moji on the Inland sea.

When completed the trunk line extending the entire length of the southern island will be 1,290 miles long. There are several branches

The Yankees of the East

connecting the important cities with the main line, one of which, from Tosu to Sada, is now being extended to Nagasaki.

On the northern island, called Yezo, there is a line 250 miles long, known as the Tonko railway, extending from Otaru, the chief city on the western coast, to Sapporo and other interior points.

The standard gauge is three feet six inches. The road beds are usually ballasted with stone, the culverts are constructed of stone and the bridges of steel. Steel rails are used, varying in weight from fifty-two to sixty-three pounds to the yard.

The usual rate of passenger trains is twenty miles an hour, and between the large cities— that is Tokyo and Yokahama, Kobe, Osaka and Kyoto—trains usually run almost every hour.

On the longer lines there is an average of four or five trains a day; generally one fast express and the others slow locals.

There are no luxuries and few comforts on the Japanese railways. There are no sleeping cars, and few of the first-class cars have toilet accommodations. Nor are there any eating houses along the line. Travelers have to carry lunch-baskets or buy the native food from the peddlers at the stations and eat it with chopsticks.

According to statistics from the Imperial

Railways and 'Rikishas

Railway Bureau, the total mileage of railways in operation at the end of March, 1895, was 2,130 miles; that of lines under construction was 1,042 miles, and the number of railway companies was twenty-nine. The following table shows the names, capital, total mileage, and mileage open to traffic of the various lines in actual operation —State railways being excluded:

Name	Capital yen.	Total Mileage Miles.	Lines open for Traffic Miles.
Nippon Tetsudo	30,000,000	799.	596.
Sanyo Tetsudo	13,000,000	307.47	191.46
Kyushu Tetsudo	11,000,000	271.01	161.05
Chikusho Tetsudo	3,700,000	38.47	30.47
Sanuki Tetsudo	330,000	10.15	10.15
Kobu Tetsudo	1,350,000	27.17	27.17
Kansai Tetsudo	6,500,000	114.22	66.53
Osaka Tetsudo	3,000,000	45.25	38.48
Hokkaido Tanko Tetsudo	6,500,000	204.71	204.71
Ryo-mo Tetsudo	1,500,000	52.17	52.17
Han-kai Tetsudo	400,000	6.13	6.13
Iyo Tetsudo	175,200	13.02	10.19
Settsu Tetsudo	240,000	8.35	8.35
Kushiro Tetsudo	200,000	26.67	26.67
Sano Tetsudo	145,000	23.58	23.58
Sangu Tetsudo	1,100,000	9.60	9.60
So-bu Tetsudo	1,200,000	31.40	31.40
Hoshu Tetsudo	2,000,000	43.65	
Nau-wa Tetsudo	500,000	16.40	
Kawagoye Tetsudo	300,000	18.40	18.40
Aoume Tetsudo	100,000	13.07	11.40
Han-tan Tutsudo	1,000,000	30.57	23.00
Nara Tetsudo	1,000,000	25.53	
Bo-so Tetsudo	350,000	11.75	
Ota Tetsudo	170,000	12.18	
Nan-yo Tetsudo	95,000	6.57	
Dogo Tetsudo	38,000	3.07	
Naniwa Tetsudo	250,000	8.13	
Hatsuse Tetsudo	500,000	12.17	
Total	86,643,203	2,193.12	1,549.39

The Yankees of the East

With regard to State Railways, figures relating to them were as follows:

Line.	Capital yen.	Total Mileage Miles.	Open for Traffic Miles.
Tokaido & Naoyetsu.	38,103,252	557.49	557.49
Fukushima-Hirosaki(Owu)	12,686,126	298.26	23.20
Tsuruga - Toyama (Hokuriku).	5,764,954	123.58	
Total	56,554,332	979.33	580.69

The grand totals for both private and State lines are as follows:

Lines	Capital yen.	Total Mileage Miles.	Open for Traffic Miles.
Private Lines	86,643,200	2,193.12	1,549.39
State Lines	56,554,332	979.33	580.69
Total	143,197,532	3,172.45	2,130.08

Freight charges on the government lines are fixed and published according to the various classifications of merchandise by an official commission, and at present are as follows:

Class 1—2 sen per picul, or 1 cent per 133 pounds per mile.

Class 2—3 sen per picul, or 1½ cents per 133 pounds per mile.

Class 3—4 sen per picul, or 2 cents per 133 pounds per mile.

Class 4—5 sen per picul, or 2½ cents per 133 pounds per mile.

Class 5—7 sen per picul, or 3 cents per 133 pounds per mile.

The government managers of the railroad

Railways and 'Rikishas

have authority to give special rates for carload lots and make contracts for large shipments, which often average as low as 1 cent per ton per mile.

There is an express service for parcels on passenger trains, charges being 1 sen (half a cent) per kin (1⅛ pounds) for 25 miles or less; 1½ sen from 25 to 50 miles, 2 sen from 50 to 100 miles and ½ sen for each additional 50 miles.

Passenger rates are as follows:

First class—3 sen (1½ cents) per mile with 133 pounds luggage.

Second class—1 sen per mile with 83 pounds luggage.

Third class—½ sen per mile with 40 pounds luggage.

On the private lines the rates are slightly higher, but are subject to government control. On short branches of the government roads there are higher charges for special rapid transit for the accommodation of suburban residents, but second-class fare is limited by law to 1½ sen (three-fourths of a cent United States gold) a mile. The highest third-class fare charged upon any of the railroads is 1.3 sen, or about 7 mills, and the lowest is 4 mills a mile.

Railway construction in Japan has been comparatively easy. There are few tunnels or heavy grades, but there is no law authorizing condem-

The Yankees of the East

nation proceedings to secure a right of way, which is often troublesome.

Numerous companies have been organized for the construction of electric railways in Japan, and many of them will doubtless carry out their plans in the immediate future.

There are also applications pending before the government for electric lines between Yokohama and Tokyo, a distance of eighteen miles, and between Kobe, Gsaka and Kyoto, forty-eight miles, where the territory is very thickly settled; but both of them propose to parallel steam railways owned by the government, and it is a question whether they will be permitted, for financial reasons. The present roads pay dividends of 9 per cent. and more into the public treasury, and their earnings would be reduced by competition.

Although Americans and other foreigners may not actively engage in the management of these enterprises, they offer a very tempting opportunity for the investment of capital, and will afford a large market for steel rails of light weight and electrical material when their construction is commenced.

The policy of the Japanese government as explained to me by the minister of agriculture and commerce, is decidedly against granting to foreigners concessions for any form of transportation or communication, or for any public im-

Railways and 'Rikishas

provements or conveniences whatsoever. He explained that the friction between the telephone, electric light, gas, water supply, railway, streetcar and similar companies and their patrons was already becoming troublesome, and that parliament would very soon be compelled to enact laws similar to those in the United States for the regulation of such enterprises. It would be much easier to control and restrict them if they are owned by citizens of Japan. Foreigners would naturally appeal for protection to the diplomatic agents of their governments, and perplexing complications might ensue. Therefore, the ministry, which had given the subject long and serious consideration, had decided, and he believed wisely, not to allow the control of any public works to be placed in the hands of foreigners. There was no objection to the investment of foreign capital in their stocks and bonds, but the management must be strictly native, and laws would probably be passed requiring all directors of such corporations to be subjects of the empire.

While the railway management in Japan is in many respects admirable, they have an aggravating way of changing the schedules of trains without the slightest notice. People never know when or why a train is taken off, or the hour of its departure postponed. Sometimes a regiment of troops coming home from the war will disar-

The Yankees of the East

range the whole service. A member of the ministry, or some high public functionary, may want to take a trip by a special, and the railway managers will take off one of the regular trains to accommodate him. Such incidents are occurring every few days, and of course some one always suffers annoyance in consequence.

One day a gentleman living in Tokyo intended to take the steamer for San Francisco, which left Yokohama at 11 o'clock. The distance is eighteen miles, and he arranged to leave by the 8:30 train, which would bring him at Yokohama at 9:20, and give him an hour and forty minutes to transfer his luggage from the railway station to the steamer. On arriving at the Tokyo station he discovered that the 8:30 train had been taken off without notice and there was no other until 10:20, which would bring him into Yokohama at 11:10, ten minutes after the hour at which his steamer was appointed to sail. He made some appropriate remarks to the railway managers at the station, and then began telegraphing all of his friends who were supposed to have influence with the steamship company. They prevailed upon the captain to wait for him, and about 11:30 he came aboard.

As a rule, however, railway officials are very obliging and take a great deal of trouble to accommodate travelers. Nor is it possible to induce them to accept a fee. In Europe a traveler

Railways and 'Rikishas

is compelled to pay everybody connected with a train or a railway station if he wants to protect himself from annoyance. He has to fee the baggagemen, the porters, the conductors, the guards and all hands, and the treatment he receives is governed by his generosity. In Japan you are expected to give a penny to the porter who carries your luggage from the jinrikisha to the baggage room, for that is his 'pidgin,' and he receives no pay from the railway, but if you offered a fee of any amount to any one else he would be grossly insulted. The same is true of policemen. As an illustration, I carelessly left a notebook on the seat of a car in which I had travelled from Tokyo to Yokohama, and did not discover my loss until the train had left for the next station. I went to the stationmaster, who immediately sent a telegram to the man in charge of the train, and I found my notebook awaiting me when I returned to the hotel at Tokyo that evening. I offered to pay the stationmaster and the telegraph operator for their trouble. They made very polite bows and assured me that they felt greatly honored by having an opportunity to do me a service, but declined to accept money.

It has been only forty years since the first steamship was seen in Japan. That was a little gunboat purchased in Holland by the Shogun Tokugawa. The example set by the regency

The Yankees of the East

was followed by several of the powerful feudal lords, like Satsuma and Saga, so that at the time of the restoration in 1868 there were ten war vessels on the coast, the largest being not more than 300 tons. Since then the Japanese navy has become powerful, and it is the intention of the government to increase it immediately to 200,000 tons.

The total strength of the navy in 1893, was thirty-two vessels, aggregating 44,777 tons, and carrying 341 guns. In 1894, at the beginning of the war, this number had been increased to thirty-five vessels, of 71,187 tons and 412 guns, At present, including the Chinese vessels captured during the war, there are now about forty-eight vessels, aggregating nearly 100,000 tons.

The following table shows the number of vessels in the merchant marine of Japan and their total and registered tonnage.

	Number.	Total Tonnage.	Registered Tonnage.
Steamers	484	299,049.92	187,387.39
Sailing vessels	186	30,726.30	28,883.20
Totals	670	329,776.22	216,270.59

The following are non-registered vessels carrying the flag of Japan:

	Number.	Tonnage.
Steamers	284	5,646
Sailing	526	13,430
Totals	810	19,076

This makes a grand total of 1,480 vessels, with a total tonnage of 348,852.22. This does

Railways and 'Rikishas

not include 17,238 junks engaged in the coasting trade, with a capacity of 2,865,759 koku. The latter term represents a measure of capacity equal to about five bushels.

The Japanese have always been a seafaring people. Their sailors are as bold and venturesome as the Norse Kings, and, as is usually the case with insular nations, have always had the most ardent taste for the sea. During the middle ages their privateers were famous and much feared among the eastern nations for their aggressiveness. They visited China, Korea, Formosa, India and the southern islands, both as peaceful traders and bucanneers. One of their sea kings, named Nagamasa, invaded Siam, married a princess and became the viceroy of that country. The story of his adventures reads like a chapter from "The Arabian Nights."

But the history of the modern Japanese navy may be said to commence with the advent of an English master mariner by the name of Will Adams, who reached the southern coast of Japan in 1600 with a Dutch fleet, and was taken prisoner and detained by the Shogun Ieyasu. He soon won the favor of that enterprising despot, and served as chief constructor in his shipyards until his death, in 1620. Although he left a wife and children in Kent county, England, he brought up a Japanese family also, and the grave of his wife and himself are still well cared

The Yankees of the East

for in the pretty cemetery near Yokosuka, a little way south of Yokohama.

Adams was the first Englishman who ever reached the shores of Japan, and under his influence the commerce of the country as well as its fighting fleet increased to considerable proportions. It is a well-authenticated fact that one of the Japanese vikings sailed as far away as the coast of Mexico; but, after the death of Adams, to check the propaganda of the catholic church inaugurated by St. Francis Xavier, the Shogun Iemitsu issued an edict by which not only all foreign priests were expelled from the country, but foreign merchants were restricted to the two southwestern ports, and Japanese subjects were forbidden to leave the country under pain of death. All of the ships that had been built under the direction of Adams were destroyed, and only junks of limited tonnage were allowed to be retained. Even they were required to be built with open sterns so that they could not go to sea. This style of junks are still seen by the thousands in the waters of Japan. They have a single square sail made of ten or twelve separate breadths strung together on cords, and when the skipper wants to shorten sail he draws up one or more of them.

For 200 years the shipping enterprise of Japan was suppressed, and it was not until 1872 that a merchant ship was owned in this country. That

Railways and 'Rikishas

year the government purchased several, which were intrusted to the management of Mr. Iwasaki Yataro, and were the nucleus of the Mitsubishi Steamship company. Later on another line was established, but the rivalry proved ruinous, and in 1885 both were amalgamated under the name of the Nippon Yusen Kaisha. In 1878 these two companies and other private owners controlled a fleet of over two hundred small coasters.

The government has been very liberal and enterprising in its encouragement of the merchant marine, and has fostered its development by liberal subsidies. Sailors are trained at government expense, not only for the navy but for the merchant service, in both engineering and navigation. The number of graduates up to last year was over 1,100, of whom fifty-four are now the commanders of steamers.

What is known as the Nippon Yusen Kaisha (Japan Mail Steamship company) is a very extensive corporation owned by Japanese capitalists, with a subsidy of $880,000 a year from the government, and special privileges of great value in the way of exemption from harbor dues and other charges. It has a monopoly of the coasting trade, and regular connections with all the Chinese ports as far south as Hong Kong, and to Korea, Siberia, Formosa and the islands of the Asiatic coast.

The Yankees of the East

It has a very large fleet of ships, which has been considerably augmented during the recent war with vessels purchased with funds loaned or at least furnished by the government. They number from eighty to ninety, from little stern-wheelers and tugboats to fine new ships of 5,000 tons. Most of their ships were formerly commanded by Englishmen and Americans and most of their chief engineers were Irish and Scotch until recently, but the managers are gradually getting rid of their foreign employes and filling their places with natives as the latter gain competency by experience. This corporation has a monopoly of the government business, and that alone would permit it to pay good dividends with the very liberal subsidy. It is, therefore, a popular and profitable corporation.

At the semi-annual meeting of the Yusen Kaisha last July the annual report of the treasurer showed a profit of $288,647 during the last six months, which was much lower than for the previous six months because of the falling off of business from the government toward the close of the war. The total for the year was $685,910 net profit, from which an annual dividend of 10 per cent, or $440,000, was paid on the capital stock of $4,400,000. The balance went to the reserve fund. The report shows that last year fifty-seven large steamers were employed, with a total of 111,342 registered tonnage and twenty-

Railways and 'Rikishas

one steamers of 57,263 tons were chartered for extra service during the war. The company also owns several small steamers for harbor service and navigation on the Inland sea. Their vessels made 603 voyages last year, aggregating 481,108 miles, and 199 voyages were made by chartered vessels, aggregating 281,073 miles. The service covered the entire Asiatic coast and the adjacent islands from Bombay, India, to Vladivostock, Siberia. The company purchased or built five steamers of a total of 14,579 tons and two of twenty-seven tons last year. Only one of their vessels met with an accident, striking a submerged rock and being badly damaged, but it was afterward raised and repaired and is now in service.

The stock of the company, which is divided into shares of 50 yen each, was quoted from 58 to 82 on 'change during the year, the average price being 76.

During the year 1895 the entire shipping of Japan was increased by seventy-seven steamers, built in the empire or purchased in foreign countries, showing a total increase in the tonnage of 123,111, of which 41,384 tons belong to the government, mostly men-of-war.

For the 'rikisha, which is the greatest blessing travelers in the east enjoy, we have to bless an American sailor who visited there on Commodore Perry's flagship in 1858, and then returned seven or

The Yankees of the East

eight years later as a missionary of the Baptist persuasion. His name was Jonathan Gobel, and he is mentioned in Commodore Perry's narrative as a pious man of rare intelligence, who took great interest in the spiritual welfare of the Japanese. Gobel was one of the earliest members of what was known as the Newton mission, a system of evangelical work inaugurated very soon after Japan was opened to foreigners by a Connecticut gentleman of that name.

The jinrikisha is another illustration of the old adage that necessity is the mother of invention, for Brother Gobel was afflicted with rheumatism in his later years and found it difficult navigate. The sedan chair which was used by the nobility was too close for him, and the kago, a vehicle in which the humbler classes were in the habit of carrying the lame and the lazy, was very uncomfortable for his long legs, so he took a packing-case, painted it black, as appropriate to his vocation, and set it upon a pair of wheels. For shelter from the sun he rigged a canvas awning that could be raised or lowered according to his convenience, and he hired a brawny coolie to haul him about. That was the origin of the vehicle which takes the place of carriages and street cars in Japan, Korea, India and China, for Brother Gobel's invention has spread all over that coast. So useful an invention needed a good name, therefore Brother Gobel called it a jin (man)

Railways and 'Rikishas

ricki (power) sha (carriage). But the swells prefer to term it a kuruma. It looks like an exaggerated baby carriage and is very comfortable for riding.

Jonathan Gobel was a muscular Christian. He feared God and lived a righteous life. He desired every one else to do so, and, when moral suasion failed, he often tried force. When he arrived in Japan he was a stalwart, powerful fellow, and usually came out uppermost when he wrestled with sin. He was living in Kanagawa when he endeavored to impress upon the people of that place the propriety of Sabbath observance. The Japanese have no Sunday. They have no fixed day of rest. Their holidays are numerous, and worship continues without interruption in the temples. There is no particular time for preaching, and it is always proper to pray. Therefore every native worked seven days in the week. Brother Gobel admonished the people of the sinfulness of Sabbath breaking, but he was unable to convince them and it grieved his heart.

Passing from his home to his place of preaching one Sunday he found a dozen men or more engaged in building a house. He stopped to talk with them and entreated them to cease their sinful labor. They refused to do so. He ordered them to stop and they declined. Then, seizing a heavy bamboo pole, he smote them hip

The Yankees of the East

and thigh. Several were laid out senseless, and the next morning Brother Jonathan was a prisoner before the consul-general, charged with aggravated assault and battery. This case appears as one of the first in the records of the United States consulate, and is set forth with amusing details. The missionary pleaded "guilty with strong provocation," and was put under bonds to keep peace.

Mr. Gobel afterward built himself a modern house on what is known as "the Bluff," south of Yokohama, and surrounded his grounds with the first fence that was ever built in that part of the world. It was made of bamboo palings, and the boys in the neighborhood used to annoy the good missionary greatly by rattling sticks against it as they ran along the street. The British admiral lived just above him and had a very natty Tommy Atkins for an orderly. He wore a little round cap on the northeast corner of his head and always carried a little cane of rattan in his hand. One morning, having been sent with a message, he appeared before the admiral with his face bruised to a jelly and his uniform tattered and torn and covered with dust.

"Mercy on us!" exclaimed the admiral, in astonishment at the spectacle, "what has happened to you?"

"I beg your parding, sir," replied Tommy, "but, has I was coming halong hup the 'ill

Railways and 'Rikishas

a-rubbing my stick hagainst the missionary's fence, sir, 'e came hout in 'is pyjamas and said as 'ow 'e 'ad vowed by the grace of God to lick the 'ide hoff the next man who did that, and 'e 'as done it, sir."

The 'rikishas are all made in Japan, and a large number are exported to the neighboring countries. They cost from $17 to $40, according to the care bestowed on their construction, the material used and the character of their decoration, but they could not be made for more than twice that money in the United States. Many of them are owned by the coolies who draw them, others by companies of private individuals who let them to the coolies for a share of the money they make. You can hire them by the week for 5 yen ($2.50), by the day for 75 sen (37½ cents), 10 sen (5 cents) an hour for ordinary service or 10 sen for a trip of not more than two miles.

The system of operating them is very much like that in use by our hackmen at home. Each 'rikisha man has his name aud number upon his hat and his lantern. He is registered at police headquarters and pays a small tax to the government. Those that are attached to the tourists' hotels are required to pay a small percentage for the privilege, as they get more patronage and many fees that do not fall to the lot of the ordinary man on the street.

The Yankees of the East

They wear a loose tunic and tights of blue or white cotton cloth that reach not quite to the knees, and are often entirely barelegged in the hot months of the summer. Sometimes on a hot day when he has to go into the country your 'rikisha man will strip down to a breech-clout. On his head he wears a hat of woven bamboo, covered with canvas, that is the shape of an inverted wash-bowl, and on his feet a pair of "waraji," or sandals woven of rice straw, that cost less than half a cent. They are made in every village and in almost every farmhouse, and the coolie usually has two or three pairs strapped to the axle of his 'rikisha, as they wear out rapidly on the gravel of the roads. In winter he goes barefooted, just as he does in the summer, with nothing but his "waraji" to protect his flesh from the snow.

The 'rikisha men are very remarkable for their endurance and many of them for their speed. I once rode twenty miles in less than three hours over a country road that had some long hills, and at the end of the journey there was scarcely a sign of weariness among the several 'rikisha men in our party. It is customary and proper on these long rides to take two men. One of them works in the shafts and the other assists by pulling on a rope made fast around his shoulders, or pushes from behind when the road is hilly. They will go fifty or sixty miles a

Railways and 'Rikishas

day for weeks at a time, and keep a gait of six miles an hour, but they expect to have one hour's rest in three. They will travel farther and faster and with less fatigue than the ordinary road horse. Their gait is an even trot, with the head and shoulders inclined forward.

The comfort of the passenger depends very much upon the way the shafts are held. If they are too high or too low he tires easily, but when the coolie gets accustomed to your most comfortable posture he will accommodate his shafts to it and you ride with less fatigue than in any carriage.

The coolies are always amiable and happy; they never get cross or stubborn, and they take great interest in their passengers. Some of them can speak a little English and make desperate efforts to explain and point out objects of curiosity along the road. Iba, who hauled me around, lived for a time in Chicago, and acquired a meager command of the dialect spoken there, which he finds very useful. Whenever a Chicago man arrives at the hotel Iba in some way finds him out and an esprit de corps is established immediately on a basis of fellow citizenship.

Gambling is prohibited in Japan under a heavy penalty. No gambling houses are allowed to exist on that island. Games of chance are always interrupted and suppressed by the police,

The Yankees of the East

and although they cannot entirely eradicate the vice or prevent its practice in the clubs of the higher classes or in the huts of the coolies, the punishment of those detected is so severe that it is less common than in any other country.

One day while we were climbing a long hill on the twenty-mile journey I have referred to, we saw a city 'rikisha man squatting on the ground ahead of us trying to interest some innocent looking countrymen in what looked like a thimble-rig game. He had spread a mat upon the ground and had some cubes of wood and little boxes which he was manipulating in a way that excited great interest in the group around him.

The 'rikisha man who led our party tried faithfully to give him a signal, for we had a detective with us. But the coolie was so interested in his game that he did not notice the warnings or perceive his danger until the officer was almost abreast of him. Then he gave a shriek of alarm and started down the hill at a gait that would have done credit to a thoroughbred race horse, leaving his paraphernalia upon the ground and his 'rikisha in the gutter. The detective made a thrust at him with the sword cane he carried, but the blow fell short, and he passed on without giving the matter any further attention; but he told us afterward that if he had been going toward the town instead of away

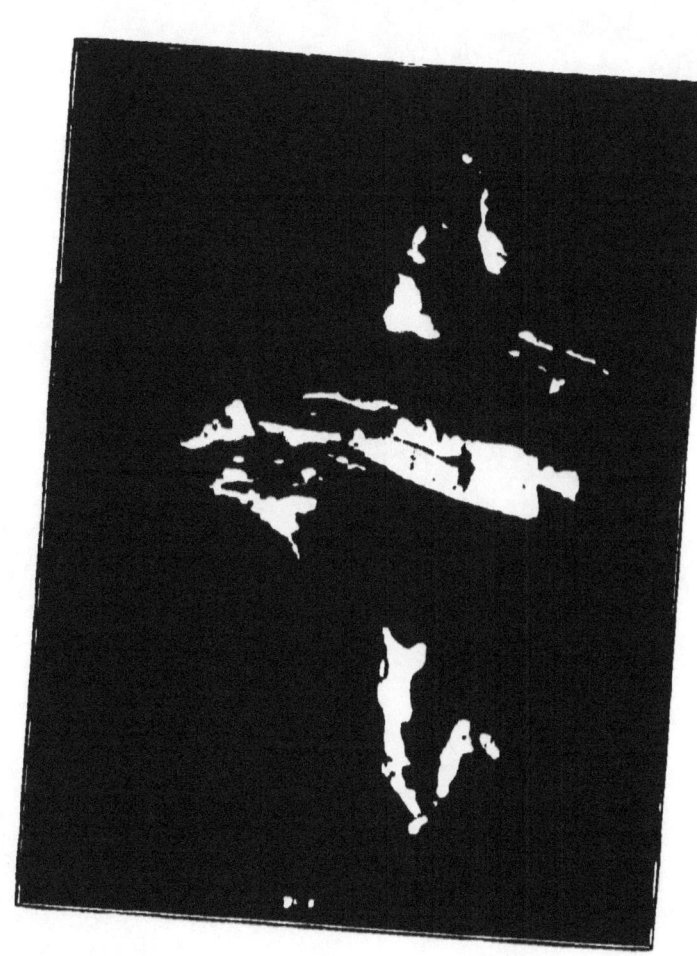

WRESTLERS READY TO SPRING.

Railways and 'Rikishas

from it he would have arrested the man, whose penalty would have been at least two months in jail and a fine of $10, which is equal to three months' pay.

Some of the 'rikisha coolies are quite elaborately tattooed. The art of tattooing has reached its highest stage in Japan, and some of the specimens one sees on the street are quite elaborate and artistic. Like everything else, the work is cheaply done. You can have a beautiful picture in colors tattooed upon your back or breast that will last a lifetime for $2 or $3, and a skillful artist, will place an indelible portrait of your lady love on your arm at about the cost of an ordinary photograph at home.

The wrestlers and the jinrikisha men of Japan upset all of the popular theories regarding training and diet. The wrestlers are the greatest gluttons in the world. They eat enormously of all forms of food—whatever is offered them—mostly vegetables and fish. They seldom eat meat, and when they do they swallow it as they do their rice, without chewing it. They drink beer, sakè, whisky and every other kind of liquor often to excess. One day at a Tokyo hotel two famous wrestlers drank two quarts of Scotch whisky with their dinner without intoxication or any other unpleasant results. They do not keep up any regular training like prize-fighters and other athletes in Europe and the United States,

The Yankees of the East

but gratify every appetite until they are satiated.

The jinrikisha men, who are remarkable for their endurance and strength, live more temperate lives, but never eat meat. They are strict vegetarians with the exception of a little dried or pickled fish, which would be indigestible in an American stomach. They eat large quantities of rice and drink gallons of tea, but they are capable of the most remarkable endurance. One night, for example, a 'rikisha man ran with me and my travelling bag in his carriage from the Uyeno railway station to the Imperial hotel, a distance of four miles, in less than half an hour. They will travel twenty-five and thirty miles at a trot without stopping to rest. They will make longer distances in less time than an ordinary horse drawing a heavy load. Their muscles are perfectly developed, but they are usually slender, while the wrestlers are very fat. The 'rikisha men are subject to heart disease, but never to diseases of the lungs or rheumatism.

They not only perform these feats in winter as well as summer, but they go about in snow-storms bare-footed and bare-legged, with nothing on their bodies but a cotton shirt, a cotton jacket and a pair of cotton trunks; yet their food contains no fat whatever and very little nitrogen, although it is rich in carbon.

Sanitary experts say that the ordinary Japa-

Railways and 'Rikishas

nese vegetable food, particularly rice, is the most healthy diet that can be adopted for persons who are accustomed to a great deal of exercise, but that it is very unhealthy to those who lead sedentary lives. At the penitentiary rice and other food is served by weight to the prisoners. Those who are engaged in hard outdoor labor like building, brickmaking and gardening are given a full quart of rice three times a day, while the potters, lacquer-workers and those engaged on cloisenne only get half as much.

VIII
The Police, the Courts and the Prisons

The Japanese policeman is the most serious and dignified person in existence. He never sits on the cellar stairs and gossips with the servant girls. He is too solemn for any such foolishness as that, and is overwhelmed with such a sense of responsibility that he cannot even smile. He is usually a small and natty person, who pays a great deal of attention to his toilet, and if he can raise a crop of whiskers, which is a luxury that all Japanese gentlemen do not enjoy, he is the ideal of complacency and the admiration of all the old women and small boys in the neighborhood.

There is no happier race on earth than the people of Japan. They are always making merry, laughing, smiling and having a good time, whether they are at work or at play. You never hear an angry word. Everybody seems to be perfectly amiable and kindly disposed toward all humanity, the animal kingdom included, for they never abuse their horses, and a jinrikisha man will always turn out of his way rather than

Police, Courts and Prisons

disturb a dog who happens to be snoozing in the middle of the road. When you hear shouts they are shouts of laughter, not of anger or distress. Cases of assault and battery are very rare in the police court, and when a man is arrested for disorderly conduct it is because he has been too joyful in his cup and disturbs the peace with merriment and not mischief.

But the policeman contemplates all this joy and amusement with a solemnity that would do credit to an Irish undertaker attending the funeral of an archbishop, as a friend has said. He permits his fellowmen and women to have a good time as long as they do not interfere with each other or disturb the peace of the community, but when it becomes necessary for him to enforce the law he does so with courtesy and consideration.

He wears a suit of blue, with a short blouse in the winter with a cap to match, and in the summer a suit of immaculate white duck, which is fresh every morning. His cap is of the same material, cut after the pattern that is common among American yachtmen. He always wears white gloves and carries a sword instead of a club; but seldom uses it, because the respect for the majesty of the law that is inborn among the Japanese usually prevents offenders from resisting arrest. He has no handcuffs, but carries in his pocket a coil of strong cord with which he

The Yankees of the East

ties the offender's hands behind him and holds the ends firmly in his own grasp, and the pair march away to the police station tandem style, with the offender about four feet ahead, and the policeman followed by a crowd of coolies and small boys and girls, every one of them with babies strapped on their backs.

An arrest is such a serious and important event that business is practically suspended in the neighborhood for the next hour or more, while the merchants discuss it with their customers and everybody else on the block, and express their views as to the penalty the prisoner ought or is likely to suffer. There are little precinct station houses at frequent intervals; neat little boxes with just room enough for a clerk and his desk, with a telephone in the corner and a big book, in which a record of business is kept with the most minute care and accuracy. When the prisoner is brought in the officer who arrested him turns in a report naming the witnesses and such details as he has gained. Then the prisoner is allowed to make a statement in explanation and give the names of persons who will testify in his behalf. He is then taken to the nearest calaboose or prison of detention to await his trial, which will take place as soon as the parties concerned can be summoned. No bail is allowed unless the inquiry is likely to be carried over several days.

Police, Courts and Prisons

Meantime the clerk at the station has telephoned headquarters, and a detective is sent out to make an investigation and summon the witnesses to appear forthwith at the courtroom, where judges are always in attendance ready to do business between eight o'clock in the morning and eight o'clock at night. No lawyers are allowed except in extraordinary cases, when the defendant is deaf and dumb, or idiotic, or for any reason is unable to give an account of himself.

The courts of Japan are not intended for litigation nor for the exhibition of legal acquirements and oratory. They exist for the purpose of ascertaining the truth and administering justice. The judge examines all the witnesses himself, and when he finds out the facts he pronounces the penalty, which is usually more severe for similar offenses than it is with us. He can send the offender to jail or to the penitentiary or to the house of correction. There is no grand jury and no appeal except where the accused has committed a serious crime. Then he is cited to a higher court and is tried immediately—just as soon as the police authorities are able to find the necessary witnesses.

If the offense is only a misdemeanor the police judge disposes of the case finally according to his own judgment and discretion upon the evidence submitted. Nor is there ever any dispute over the admissibility of evidence. The object being to ascertain the truth, the judge examines everybody who knows anything about the case, whether it is direct or hearsay testimony. He is supposed to be strictly impartial, and weighs the evidence in his own mind, giving due allowance to passions and prejudices and the relations of witnesses. He is supposed to know that a wife or a mother will present the most favorable side of the controversy, and that an enemy will do everything he can to injure.

The prisoner is allowed to make a statement for himself or through some friend or attorney, but if he is a man of intelligence the court usually exercises its discretion and requires him to speak for himself. If the offense is a felony the defendant is sent directly to a higher court having jurisdiction over such crimes without preliminary trial, and is prosecuted by the official procurator, who is prosecuting attorney and grand jury combined.

A person who has suffered injury by crime makes complaint at a police station or to the procurator, when a warrant is issued upon his affidavit and the arrest is made. Bail is allowed at the discretion of the court upon the recommendation of the procurator. The accused is allowed the benefit of counsel, but the judge alone can examine witnesses.

The detective service of Japan is admirable,

ENTRANCE TO THE SHRINE OF IEYASU, NIKKO.

Police, Courts and Prisons

and is inherited from the days of despotism, when it was necessary for the shogun to know everything that was going on among his subjects. There are two distinct detective agencies under the government, one being connected with the ordinary police for the prevention and punishment of crime, and the other being political, under the department of the interior.

The latter showed its efficiency during the late war, for the Japanese knew more about the Chinese army, its fortresses, its arms and equipments and the condition of the navy than Li Hung Chang himself. The agents of the intelligence department were not only ingenious and indefatigable, but a mass of valuable information was received at headquarters from volunteer spies and from persons who had visited China recently and knew facts of value to their government.

The intelligence department has so complete a system that it claims to be aware of everything that is going on in the empire, and I presume that is true, particularly in politics. The criminal department of the police is equally industrious and efficient. In the first place every citizen, man, woman and child, in Japan is registered at police headquarters, with his residence, his occupation, and even the wages he receives, if he is a workman or an employé. Whenever he changes his abode, his occupation or his place

The Yankees of the East

of employment he is required to notify the registrar and a correction is made upon the books. Every hotel is required to report the arrival and departure of its guests as promptly as possible, with the places they came from, the train they take, and their destination. Therefore it is easy for the police to ascertain the whereabouts of any person at any time, and they have a good starting point to work from when they are inquiring into a case.

Not long since, for illustration, Mr. Miller, official interpreter of the United States legation in Tokyo, failed to receive a letter which was sent him from a neighboring city with a draft inclosed, and he notified the police. The detective assigned to the case began by ascertaining the day and hour when the letter was posted, from which he could easily calculate the exact time of its arrival Tokyo. By reference to the register at headquarters he found that there were two persons named Miller in the city, although their initials were different and they lived far apart. The postmen who served the district in which they lived were questioned, and one of them remembered delivering a letter to the house of the wrong Miller on the date named. Several members of the family recalled that such a letter that did not belong to them had been received, and one of the servants reported that she had handed it to a peddler who had agreed to put it in the nearest post box and save her the trouble. The peddler was found and identified by the servant. His premises were searched and the money was discovered concealed under the matting of the floor. He had forged an endorsement and got the draft cashed by a merchant, who had sent it to his bank for collection in the regular course of business. These facts were all ascertained and the thief was sentenced to four years' imprisonment within a week after Mr. Miller made his complaint to the police.

Mr. James R. Morse, of Yokohama, happened to be spending the night with his friend, Mr. Denison, in Tokyo, when a sneak thief entered the house and stole his pocketbook containing $70 and a number of valuable papers. The matter was reported to the police in the morning with a description of the purse and its contents, and within forty-eight hours the papers were recovered and the thief had begun a term of six years imprisonment at Ishikawa, the national penitentiary.

The process of his detection was very prompt and simple. The crime was reported at police headquarters at eight o'clock in the morning. By nine the theft and description of the property had been telephoned to every precinct in the city and to all the suburban towns and were known to every officer on duty. In a little vil-

The Yankees of the East

lage about ten miles from the center of Tokyo a man entered a tea house during the afternoon and showed a card upon which Mr. Morse's name was engraved. Tea houses in Japan correspond with saloons in the United States as resorts for loafers and the crooked classes, and the policemen watch them accordingly. The nesans, as the waiter girls are called, coquet with the policemen and often aid them in the performance of their duty. So it was perfectly natural for the policeman on that beat to tell the nesans the story of the robbery and it was equally so for this nesan to report to the policeman about Mr. Morse's card. The circumstance was suspicious enough to justify an arrest and before night the thief was in the central station at Tokyo. He had the pocketbook and all the papers on his person, but had spent the most of the money in a spree the night before and had been robbed of the remainder during a drunken stupor that followed.

I saw a good deal of the Japanese detective corps while Mr. Foster was in Japan. As he had been connected with the Chinese government, and his face and name were so well known to the public through their frequent appearance in the illustrated papers, it was feared lest some fanatic or soshi might attack him, therefore the government without consulting Mr. Foster instructed the police department to keep him under constant surveillance while he was in the country. All of the foreign legations are constantly watched by the police, and a detective with a jinrikisha is always on duty opposite them to follow members of the diplomatic corps wherever they go.

Mr. Foster was sometimes attended by five detectives. The superintendent of police at Kobe went with him as far as Kyoto, and the Kyoto superintendent of police as far as Nagoya, as a mark of respect, and although he protested against these attentions and assured the authorities repeatedly that he had not the slightest apprehension of danger, they replied that they held themselves responsible for his safety while in Japan, and must insist upon maintaining the guard. Sometimes while he was in Tokyo and Yokohama Mr. Foster succeeded in eluding his shadows, much to their chagrin, but they very soon discovered that he had outwitted them and ascertained his whereabouts in some mysterious manner, which showed their efficiency. One night he slipped out of the hotel by the back door to call on a friend, and managed to reach his destination without being overtaken, but at the conclusion of the visit as he was starting homeward he found a half-dozen detectives sitting coolly around the door. How they discovered his whereabouts is a mystery, for no one knew where he was going, and he left the hotel unobserved.

As a rule the young men of Japan are temperate and well behaved. They are industrious, polite and particularly deferential to their elders. They have clubs and other resorts, but tea houses are the usual scenes of dissipation. When a young rake wants to sow a few wild oats he gives a dinner at a tea house, provides an adequate supply of sakè, the native drink, and his party sit around on the floor with their food in bowls and upon trays before them shouting louder and louder as their blood becomes inflamed with the liquor. Five or six geisha dancers are then called in to entertain them with songs and dances and the proprietor of the tea house sends them home in 'rikishas when the carousal is over.

One of the greatest objections raised to the recent treaties made with Japan by the United States and European powers was the unwillingness of foreign residents in the empire to intrust the protection of their personal and property rights to the native courts, on the ground that they were not sufficiently enlightened and impartial to render fair and just judgments in disputes between natives and foreigners. Under the shoguns the legislative, executive and judicial powers of the government

TOMB OF ICYASU, THE GREAT SHOGUN.

Police, Courts and Prisons

were not distinct, and various officials did not hesitate to exercise all three, and settle all differences and disputes that occurred within their provinces. There was no notion of legislative power as we understand it. Three hundred years ago Ieyasu, the great shogun, compiled what is known as "The One Hundred Laws," which related chiefly to the relations between the sovereign and the subject, and were considered as wise as the utterances of Solomon. Other affairs were regulated by custom or by decrees of the emperor, which, however, were rare. The shogun had direct control at the capital and over the five provinces that surrounded it, and in the distant provinces the feudal princes or daimyos had absolute authority, each in his own territory, although finally responsible to the shogun.

The idea of judicial power was feebly developed and was limited almost exclusively to criminal jurisdiction. There were criminal courts, but no civil courts. There were two departments of police called gyo-bu-sho and danp-dai. The minister of justice exercised supervision over ordinary criminal affairs, heard appeals from the criminal courts, appointed all the judges, and often instructed them how to decide if they were in doubt or if there were any political significance to the case. He had power also to remove them at will, according to their behavior, so that the

The Yankees of the East

limited judicial system of the empire was actually under despotic control.

The gyo-bu-sho were the city police, responsible for public order, the public health, the suppression of crime and the protection of property.

The danp-dai were political police, and consisted of a very closely organized corps of inspectors, who looked after the integrity and efficiency of public officials, saw that the taxes were properly collected and honestly expended and investigated charges of disloyalty among the people. There is a similar institution in nearly every civilized country, but in Japan, under the shogun, the secret police were remarkably active and efficient.

With other reforms adopted by the government after the restoration of the mikado's power the French system of jurisprudence was introduced, with a minister of justice at its head, who exercises functions similar to those of the corresponding officer in France. The government is represented in the courts by procurators, who are inspectors, grand juries and prosecuting attorneys in all matters which concern the public welfare. They initiate all criminal proceedings and conduct them down to the execution of the sentence. As in France, the judge not only presides in court but conducts the trials. The lawyers have very little part in them. The de-

Police, Courts and Prisons

fendant in a criminal case, or either party to a civil proceeding, may employ counsel to advise him and appear with him in court. The counsel may not, however, examine witnesses or take any other part in the proceedings except to make statements of facts in behalf of their clients and deliver arguments pointing out to the court the favorable portions of the testimony and citing appropriate precedents and sections of law. If the lawyer thinks the court is not getting at the kernel of the case from the witnesses he may suggest questions, writing them on a slip of paper and passing them up to the judge, who may use his discretion in putting them to the witness, but the attorney cannot entrap or confuse a witness, nor object to any line of testimony that the judge desires to pursue.

By many of the ablest lawyers in Japan this is considered the weak spot in the system. There are practically no rules of evidence; no distinction is made between direct and hearsay or direct and circumstantial evidence. The object of the court is to obtain as much information as it can concerning the matter at issue, and every fact bearing upon the case is adduced, from whatever source it comes, although husband and wife, parents and children, masters and servants may not be compelled to testify against each other. The judge is then supposed to weigh the evidence in his own mind, making proper allowances for partiality and prejudice, and to reach a conclusion as to the truth. But this plan is based upon the assumption that the judges are wise, discreet and familiar with human nature, which is not always true.

And if there is no written law to cover a case the judge is supposed to exercise his common sense, being governed in a measure also by the customs of the country and previous decisions that may be regarded as precedents. Legislation has been abundant since parliament was introduced in Japan. In fact, many people think it has been excessive. A gentleman who has been here many years and has witnessed the development of Japan, remarked: "The leaders of the reform here have seemed to think that schools and acts of parliament were all that were necessary to redeem and regenerate this country. The result has been over-education and an enormous amount of legislation which is ambiguous and contradictory."

But there are codes in preparation which simplify complications, harmonize contradictions and clear up ambiguities.

Many of the present judges were trained in the feudal courts under the shoguns. They have mature age, experience and a thorough acquaintance with Japanese human nature, and in criminal cases are said to give better satisfaction than the younger generation of the judiciary, who

Police, Courts and Prisons

have graduated at the Imperial university or from law schools in Europe and America. The university, curiously enough, has three departments of law. One based upon English, one upon French and one upon German jurisprudence. There are also private law schools, one having as many as 2,500 students.

The chief justice of the Supreme court is appointed by the emperor for his learning, his ability and other special qualifications. The remaining seats upon the bench down to the lowest grade are filled by competitive examinations and promotion. Every year a commission, composed of the chief justice, a representative of the department of justice, two or three professors from the law schools and such members of the higher judiciary as may be designated, sits for the examination of candidates for the bench. Graduates of the law department of the Imperial university and recognized institutions in foreign countries are eligible upon application and are put through a very severe series of tests to ascertain their learning and fitness. Those who attain a certain standard are certified to the minister of justice and are appointed by him as probationary judges. They have no regular duties on the bench, and are allowed to continue the practice of law, but are called upon whenever necessary to assist the regular judges in the performance of their duties, to act as substitutes when temporary vacancies occur and often have cases referred to them for investigation in chambers when the regular courts are crowded with business. They also exercise functions similar to those of masters in chancery, commissioners and notaries public. In other words, they are apprentices in the judiciary system for the purpose of obtaining practical experience before assuming the responsibilities of regular judges.

Most of them have only a theoretical education and are entirely without experience at the bar. When a vacancy occurs on the bench it is filled by promotion, after a severe examination of candidates, from the next lowest grades, and vacancies in the very lowest grade are filled by competitive examination among the probationaries. In this examination a man's record is always carefully investigated, and many of the lower judges whose decisions have been frequently overruled by the higher courts do not dare appear as candidates for promotion lest they be rejected.

All judges are appointed for life or good behavior, and are removable only after trial by impeachment before a court of their superiors. Their salaries are amazingly small. The chief justice receives 8,000 yen, which is equivalent to $4,000. His associates in the Supreme court receive but 5,000 yen. The next lower grade,

Police, Courts and Prisons

which corresponds to our federal circuit judges, are paid 4,000 yen, and the others proportionately less down to the lowest grade, where the salaries are only 700 yen or $350 a year. The probationaries do not receive a regular salary, but are paid by the job, usually 5 yen a day for the time they are employed.

The judiciary does not rank as high socially as members of the military and naval service—nor in fact do any of the civil functionaries. A sergeant of marines outranks a school teacher, and the champion wrestler is regarded in public opinion as a greater man than a successful poet, author or artist. Nor are marks of distinction conferred upon members of the bar. The sons of gentlemen look down upon professional careers and prefer to seek positions in the naval and military service or in the executive department of the government.

The judiciary is, however, absolutely free from interference by the executive and legislative branches. There was a rather interesting controversy not long ago between the minister of justice and a judge of the court at Nagasaki who was transferred to the Loochoo islands without consultation. He refused to go on the ground that the law stipulates that judges shall serve for life in the districts to which they are originally assigned, except upon application, whereupon the minister of justice suspended him.

The Yankees of the East

He appealed to the prime minister and demanded an investigation, which was granted, but before it took place he relieved the government from a perplexing controversy by dying of typhoid fever.

As I have observed in previous chapters, the Japanese people are easy to rule. They are very obedient to authority. They have not only been in a state of subjection for centuries, but each child from the moment its intelligence begins to develop is taught respect for and submission to the head of the family. This respect becomes reverence when applied to the emperor, who is the head of all families, and is shared by whoever represents him.

The people are not litigious. They usually settle their affairs among themselves. Nor are they quarrelsome. They seldom lose their tempers. You never see a fight upon the streets. They are the most amiable nation on the earth and there are no profane words in their language. But at the same time they are often exasperating, and an honest Yankee remarked the other day that he would much prefer to live in a country "where people kiss and cuss" rather than in Japan, where they do neither. They are great thieves, and the most prevalent crimes are burglary, larceny, and obtaining money under false pretenses. Very few Japanese firms have regular solicitors, and they will not go to law

Police, Courts and Prisons

unless compelled to do so by unscrupulous opponents.

In Japanese courts there is always an air of great solemnity. The judges—and in the higher courts there are always three—wear gowns of black, embroidered with white braid in peculiar geometric patterns around the collar and down the front and back. Each grade of the judiciary has its distinguishing pattern, and the more braid you see on a judge's gown the higher his rank. They also wear a cap of black silk of a peculiar pattern that looks like a liberty cap.

The lawyers wear similar caps and gowns, but with a different design in the ornamentation. Their caps resemble those of the Kirghis of Russia, and have ribbons falling down behind. The embroidery indicates the rank or classification of practitioners, who are divided according to the French system, into solicitors, barristers, notaries, etc.

When addressing the court, the lawyers stand before small tables with pens and ink upon them and papers and books which they need for reference and bring into court in small satchels, instead of green bags as the English use. In the higher courts they present briefs and arguments in writing which they are required to read. The judge occasionally asks questions, and the attorneys are allowed to make oral explanations, but they are expected to re-

The Yankees of the East

duce their explanations to writing afterward if they have any important bearing upon the points at issue.

The clerk of the court sits at the right of the bench, and behind him there is always a young officer in uniform who is supposed to represent the emperor. A few rude benches furnish accommodations for clients and spectators, but the judicial proceedings do not often attract a crowd.

There is a Bar association in Japan, but so far no scale of fees has been fixed and charges for legal services are very much lower than in the United States and Europe. Many lawyers do not make more than fifty cents a day, the usual earnings of a jinrikisha man, and few of them have incomes exceeding $200 or $300 a year. There are, however, exceptions, as in the case of Mr. Masujima, who has an extensive practice among foreigners and corporations, employs a large staff of assistants, and has an income equal to that of many of the foremost lawyers in the United States. There are several law journals, but no official reports. Mr. Masujima publishes a digest of the decisions of the higher courts as a private enterprise.

I spent a very pleasant evening in Tokyo last summer at the residence of the Hon. Miyoshi Taizo, the distinguished chief justice of the Imperial Supreme court of Japan, with a

Police, Courts and Prisons

party of philanthropists who are contemplating the organization of a Prisoners' Reform association. That will be another step in the progress of a nation which, from the war previous to its recent struggle with China, brought back as trophies more than 3,000 human ears, cut from the heads of prisoners, but sent to Korea with its army a year ago a regiment of young women clad in a neat white uniform and wearing the well-known broad scarlet emblem upon the left sleeve which marks the members of the Society of the Red Cross. These "ministering angels" showed no distinction in their attendance upon the wounded of their own army and those of the enemy, and the admirable hospital corps, which was equipped with all the appliances that medical science could apply, healed the sick and bound the injuries of the Chinese as well as the Japanese. The Chinese army has no medical corps and carries no medical stores. As a distinguished Chinaman at Tientsin remarked, they found it less trouble to get fresh and healthy soldiers than to heal the wounded and cure the sick; so they left the former on the battlefield and the latter lying by the roadside as they fled before the victorious troops of Japan.

There was a curious story which I am told is true, that the emperor, having obtained relief from some ailment by the use of patent pills that were sent him from Europe, ordered 400 pounds of that remedy through a Tientsin druggist, and shipped them to Korea to be distributed among the Chinese troops. But they never reached their destination. Some skeptical or superstitious mandarin had them dumped into the sea.

The reports of the medical corps of the Japanese army show that its surgeons treated more sick and wounded Chinese than Japanese soldiers; but it should be said in this connection that the casualties among the latter were much less than among their enemies. The actual number of Japanese soldiers killed in battle during the nine months of active hostilities was only 632, and 172 died from wounds. Those who died from disease, mostly cholera, were 2,489, so that the total casualties of the war were 3,284.

Chief Justice Miyoshi is a Christian convert, a member of the Congregational church, president of the Young Men's Christian association and an active leader in all the charitable movements that are going on in Japan. He was educated in Germany and England, and is a personal friend of the emperor, who selected him from among the imperial judiciary for the distinguished post he now adorns.

The present prison system of Japan is modeled upon the most approved of modern methods for correction and reform, but nothing has

Police, Courts and Prisons

thus far been done to promote the welfare of discharged convicts and protect them from the temptation to return to lives of crime. But it is now proposed to organize a society for that purpose, and an inquiry is being conducted to obtain plans and suggestions from associations in other countries which have had experience in this form of benevolence.

There are two great prisons in Tokyo for the confinement of offenders who are sentenced for short terms by the courts of that province. Those who are condemned for life or for more than ten years are sent to the convict station in Yezo, the northern island of the empire, where they are under the care of Christian missionaries, but the short-term prisons at Tokyo, and those in other parts of the country, conducted upon the same plan, are open to the clergy of all religions—Christians, Buddhists and Shintoists. The greater prison of Tokyo is situated upon the island of Ishikawa, in an estuary of the bay, south of the city, and there is a special prison for the reformation of women called Ichigaya in the northern portion of the capital. The former is completely isolated and surrounded by high walls. The only means of reaching it is by a boat that is operated by the police and leaves its dock at intervals for the convenience of officials and visitors.

When I visited the place there were 2,848

The Yankees of the East

men and boys over the age of sixteen serving sentences ranging from six months to ten years. In 1894 there were 3,711 names upon the prison rolls, many having been discharged during the year. Of these, 1,737 had more or less education and could read and write; 1,973 were entirely uneducated. Those who had a regular occupation numbered 3,366; those who had none were only 345. Those who owned property numbered 597; the remainder had none. The prisoners in confinement were sentenced for the following crimes:

Forgery of coin and government bank bills	9
Forgery of official documents	8
Forgery of private documents	165
Homicide	21
Larceny	770
Burglary	58
Assault and battery	99
Forfeited bonds to keep the peace	89
Obtaining money under false pretenses	599
Intruding upon private premises	30
Total	2,848

The prison consists of thirty or more detached buildings of a single story, used as offices, workshops, hospitals and dormitories. The latter are enormous wooden cages made of square bars about four inches thick, which accommodate ninety-six convicts each, who sleep upon thick quilts called futons, laid on the matted floor in the ordinary Japanese style, and are entirely surrounded by narrow corridors in

Police, Courts and Prisons

which armed sentinels pace to and fro incessantly during the night. There is not an article of furniture in the entire structure, but everything is as neat as a New England kitchen, and the unpainted woodwork is polished until it shines like glass. In the morning the futons are rolled up and stored away upon a wide shelf that hangs around the walls below the ceiling. The sanitary arrangements are perfect, and the health reports show little sickness and few deaths. The hospitals are clean and cheerful; each prisoner is required to take a hot bath every night, and the food, which is cooked in the common kitchen, is regulated by dietary rules established by a medical commission. It is the ordinary food of the native Japanese, and chiefly vegetables, rice, bean soup, preserved fish and other wholesome articles, which are served in rations. The prisoners who are engaged at hard labor are furnished twice as much as those that have sedentary duties, and when a man is given active employment his ration is increased.

The only method of punishment is solitary confinement in a wooden cell, which can be lightened or darkened by the attendant, according to the disposition of the inmate. Those who are refractory are chained to the floor and fed upon bread and water until they are subdued. But the Japanese are a docile people,

The Yankees of the East

fond of society and love light; so that a few days of solitude in dense darkness, with nothing to eat but dry bread, soon brings the most stubborn offender to terms.

The prisoners wear a uniform of red cotton. They are organized into battalions of ninety-six and subject to the strictest military discipline, being drilled both night and morning to teach them obedience, regularity and precision. There are a dozen or more workshops in which they labor nine hours each day in various kinds of employment. Those who have trades are placed in the shops where they can be most useful. Those who have none are taught by skillful superintendents. Some of the work is done under contract of Tokyo firms. The products of non-contract labor are sold at auction. There are machine-shops, brick-yards, lacquer and cloisonne shops, furniture and basket factories, potteries and various other mechanical industries, and studios for decorative art in which some excellent work is done.

The prisoners are credited with the results of their labor, and upon their discharge are given in cash one-tenth of the proceeds of its sale, so that when a long-time convict is discharged he has a supply of funds at his disposal to support him until he can find honest employment. In case a considerable sum is due him it is paid in

Police, Courts and Prisons

installments by an agent of the prison commission in order that he may not be robbed or spend the money in dissipation.

At the end of his term, however, an adult convict is detained six months in the prison unless his family appear to reclaim him, and during the detention he wears a blue uniform and is employed at wages about the institution. Convicts under age are detained until they reach their majority unless their friends reclaim them in the meantime. Discharged convicts are required to report at police headquarters once in three months for a term of three years and give an account of themselves, and give prompt notice to the police whenever they change their residence or place of employment. If they fail to do so they are arrested and punished. Those who habitually neglect this requirement are sent back to prison for a violation of the law. They are really ticket-of-leave men for three years after their discharge, but, as a matter of fact, the police never lose sight of them. A discharged convict is always under surveillance until he has recovered his reputation and has proved his purpose to lead an honorable life.

About two-thirds of the present inmates of Ishikawa are old offenders — habitual criminals — for crime in Japan is almost an incurable disease, as it is in other countries. But the habitual

The Yankees of the East

offenders are mostly thieves and swindlers, who endeavor to make a living by their wits. Swindling is the prevailing crime in Japan.

The woman's prison at Ichigaya is very much like that in which male criminals are confined upon the island. The women convicts wear a similar uniform and are treated in a similar manner. The average number of inmates is about 300, who are usually sentenced for larceny; and most of them are old offenders. The officials say that it is difficult to reform a wicked woman. They are employed at light labor — weaving, spinning, sewing and embroidering, and do some very good work.

The term "suri" is used in Japan to describe professional thieves, pickpockets, sneak thieves, pocket-book snatchers, kleptomaniacs, and such classes of people. The total number of professional suri entered upon the dockets of the police of Tokyo since the records were commenced in 1884 is 1,162, of whom about five per cent are women. During the year 1894, 494 pickpockets and sneak thieves were arrested, of whom only two were women. The police authorities told me that the total number of suri at the capital, which has a population of nearly a million and a half, is about 500.

The suri, like almost every other occupation in Japan, are organized into guilds, which have

Police, Courts and Prisons

apportioned the city among its members, under the direction of about seventy masters of the trade. All of the masters are ostensibly engaged in honest business, but are known to the police. Most of them are grog-shop keepers, but some are tailors and small merchants. The relations between the masters and the disciples of the suri began hundreds of years ago, and flourished in the days of the Shoguns, but since the adoption of the modern police system it has been more difficult for them to preserve it. When the disciple brings in plunder, the master disposes of it for him, and serves as a "fence," as the police term it in this country. When a thief is arrested and, thrown into prison the master provides him food, blankets and other comforts, and employs a lawyer and witnesses to help him out of the scrape.

There is an underground connection between the police and the masters of the suri, by which both gain advantages. For example, the police will be perfectly willing to overlook the peccadillos of small offenders provided the suri will assist them in apprehending those who have committed serious crimes. Reciprocity of this kind is carried on in Japan just as it is in America. When a disciple deserts his chief, and starts business on his own hook, or when a thief who belongs in one district poaches on the preserves

The Yankees of the East

of his neighbor, or when a professional sharper from the country comes into town and endeavors to ply his trade, the police find no difficulty in catching him, and they are supposed to get their clues from the jealous suri.

The suri are divided into three classes according to the special lines they pursue. The Japanese who wear the old-fashioned dress—and ninety-nine per cent of them still do so—have no pockets in their kimonos, but use their sleeves and girdles for the same purpose. Therefore the term pickpocket scarcely applies; but one class of the suri devote their talents entirely to robbing people on the streets of watches, purses and other valuables that are thrust into their belts or sleeves, or the loose bosom of the kimono. The second class are sneak thieves that in the day time plunder tea houses and residences of people who leave valuables exposed. The third are those who hold up men and women in the street, and really commit highway robbery. The latter are considered the more honorable. Japanese pickpockets are very skillful, and their dexterity is often equal to that of a sleight-of-hand juggler. Sneak thieves often carry chloroform with them, and then, entering a house or shop, cleverly apply a sponge or a cloth saturated with the drug to the person who happens to be in charge.

Police, Courts and Prisons

The beggars too have a guild, although they are very few, and are only found about the temples. Their chief or oyakata, as they call him, is often a man in comfortable circumstances, who allots stands to the various mendicants, and receives a percentage of what they collect. But no one need be a beggar in Japan except from choice. Those who stand around the temples are professionals who select this sort of employment rather than do honest labor, because benevolence, being one of the highest virtues recognized by the Buddhist religion, the worshippers who come and go throw pennies into their boxes not so much to benefit them as to receive the credit due generous alms-givers on the books of the recording angel.

Temple mendicants are sometimes decrepid priests who are allowed to take stations, and earn their living in that way.

Another curious guild is that of the food-peddlers — men who go about the streets selling vegetables, fish and other articles of food. They are organized under a oyakata, and each has his streets allotted to him, outside of which he is not permitted to sell his wares. The oyakata receives a fee or percentage upon the sales for protecting the peddler with the police and preventing interference from outside sources, and there being a large number of them they have

The Yankees of the East

the city divided into equal portions, so that each may have his own jurisdiction. Any intruder from the outside is soon made to feel the force of the guild's resentment.

While these peculiar guilds are not recognized as lawful by the authorities they have the tacit protection of the police because they are useful in preventing collisions between rival hucksters, and preserving the peace.

MADAME CHRYSANTHEMUM AT HOME.

IX
Marriage and Divorce

When a young man wants to get married in Japan he does not offer his heart and hand to the girl he loves, but, if an arrangement has not already been made for him by his parents with the daughter of a neighbor, he goes to a discreet and trusted friend who is already married, and asks that he and his wife act as "nakodos," or go-betweens for him in this important matter. It is the most delicate duty one friend can perform for another; it is the highest of compliments to ask it, as it is naturally an evidence of complete confidence, and the gentleman and lady who undertake it assume responsibilities that few people in America would care to accept. They not only agree to find a suitable partner for the aspirant for matrimonial honors, but remain through life in the relation of godfather and godmother to the young couple. They are expected to assist them if they get into difficulty or suffer misfortune, to promote their prosperity and happiness in all ways possible, and serve as a board of arbitration to settle disputes that may arise in the family.

The Yankees of the East

But this responsibility is not dreaded in Japan as much as would be supposed. People are used to it, and nearly every gentleman and lady of acknowledged distinction have at least one and sometimes several couples under their care.

As a rule, in the upper circles of society marriages between the sons and daughters of friendly families are arranged by the parents when the children are very young, and a boy or girl often know who they are going to marry long before they are old enough to understand the nature of that relation. But they are not allowed to associate with each other. From infancy girls are taught that they are inferior to their brothers, and must treat them with respect accordingly. A boy can call his sister by a pet name, but she cannot show the same familiarity toward him. He is "Ani-san," which literally means " Mr. Brother," and his authority cannot be disputed in their play. Confucius taught that children of seven years should be separated, but the Japanese are a little more liberal than the Chinese in this respect, and boys and girls play together until they are ten or twelve years of age. After that their association is forbidden.

Nor is there any opportunity for a boy to become acquainted with the girls of his father's set. Therefore courting is impossible, and the children of families whose houses may adjoin grow up as strangers to each other. This rule

Marriage and Divorce

applies equally to the nearest relations. There can be no friendship between young men and women. It is disreputable for a Japanese young man to marry for love. When a young man and a young woman love each other public sentiment places them very low in the scale of morals.

The social laws of Japan require that people shall marry at the age of eighteen or nineteen, and it is a disgrace for a man or a woman to remain single after they are twenty or twenty-one. As a consequence there are very few old bachelors or old maids in the empire.

But a young man usually has an opportunity to inspect the girl selected by his parents or his nakodos before an engagement is decided upon, and if either is dissatisfied with the appearance of the other the arrangement may be declared off. This meeting is called a "mi-yai," which means literally "mutual seeing."

According to etiquette the interview may take place at the residence of the nakodos or at the house of the young lady's father; but among the lower classes a picnic or a theater party, a boat ride or an excursion of some sort serves the purpose. If the visit takes place at the house of the young lady's father, the young man and his nakodo are received by the host and salute each other with great politeness. A servant brings a pot of tea and materials for

The Yankees of the East

smoking, over which the three gentlemen discuss politics, business matters, the condition of the rice market, the news from China, or any other indifferent subject for a while. Then the host will clap his hands and the young lady in interest herself appears, dressed in her prettiest kimono and obi and bearing a tray containing three cups and a pot of tea. These she places upon the mat in front of the guests and proceeds to serve the beverage and sweetmeats which her mother or a servant brings after her. Girls are trained to perform this duty with the greatest degree of grace, for tea-pouring is regarded as the highest accomplishment a Japanese woman can acquire, and this occasion is naturally of the greatest importance. She is not to speak unless she is spoken to, and the responsibility of beginning a conversation with her rests upon the nakodo. If he is a gentleman of tact he introduces some subject or asks some question that is calculated to bring out whatever conversational powers the young lady may possess, and in the meantime she sits upon her heels and endeavors to be as charming as possible. The young man may engage in the conversation, but it is not good form for him to address his remarks to her. He may speak to her father or her mother, but usually remains entirely silent during the ordeal. If the "miyai" happens to be an excursion or a theater

Marriage and Divorce

party, the same rule is observed. He may look as much as he likes, but it is bad manners for him to show the young lady any particular attention.

After the mi-yai is over the young man and his nakodo retire for consultation. He thinks the matter over, and if he decides that the candidate is acceptable his parents send her a handsome box of gifts. Sometimes it contains silks and other fabrics, ornaments or jewelry, decorative works of art, and, among the common people, fish, seaweed and delicate forms of food. Then the bride's parents send presents in return, which is equivalent to an engagement, and an early day is selected for the wedding. If the young lady should happen to object, which is not often the case, as she is guided entirely by the wishes of her parents in this and all other matters, the nakodo is notified before an opportunity to send presents is given.

When the day for the wedding is selected the trousseau of the bride and several articles of household furniture are sent to her husband's home, and they are usually exhibited to the friends of the family beforehand. The wedding gown is always pure white, and the bridegroom is dressed in a "kamishimo"—a peculiar dress made of various kinds of silk in colors according to his rank.

The wedding ceremony takes place at the

The Yankees of the East

house of the bridegroom's parents, and friends of both families are invited to attend. The bride is escorted there at nightfall by her parents and other members of her family and the nakodos, followed by servants bearing gifts to the family of the bridegroom. It was formerly the custom to light a bonfire in front of the gate of her parental home and lift her over it. This ceremony signified purification. The house of the bridegroom is usually decorated with lanterns and other evidences of festivity, which draw all the people in that part of town to witness the bride's arrival. She is met outside the entrance by the members of the groom's family, but he remains seated on a cushion in front of the tokonoma, a shallow recess or alcove that is found in all Japanese houses, and is used for the display of ornaments. When she enters the room she is escorted to a seat beside him. The nakodos sit at his right and at her left are usually two married ladies or two little girls dressed in white, who serve as bridesmaids.

When the party is thus placed a chorus of voices in the adjoining room sings a Japanese song called "Utai." A low table of white wood, that has never been used, is then brought in and a tray is placed upon it containing three cups, which one of the bridesmaids fills with saké. The latter hands the smallest cup to the bride, who takes three dainty sips of wine and

Marriage and Divorce

then passes it to the groom, who follows her example.

The second and third cups are filled in a similar manner, and the ceremony is repeated. As the groom returns the third cup to the bridesmaid all clap their hands, which is a salute or approbation announcing that the ceremony is over.

There is no kissing or embracing, but a great many congratulations are offered to the young couple and guests of literary attainments are expected to hand them poems of their own composition, which are afterward bound in a little book as a memento of the occasion. The couple then retire to put off the wedding robes and resume their ordinary garments, and afterward join the guests at a feast, which is served with great ceremony. The congratulations are there renewed and include the parents and relatives of the couple, and everybody drinks to the health of the bride and groom. Sometimes the feasting continues very late, and often ends in a carousal, but before the guests retire they repeat their congratulations, as is customary in other countries.

Among the common people the marriage ceremony is considerably modified. Bridesmaids are omitted and the nakodos, the gentleman sitting at the right of the groom and his wife at the left of the bride, fill and pass the cups of

The Yankees of the East

saké; but there is always a supper of some kind and plenty to drink, if the food is only rice and salted fish and the liquids only tea.

When the guests have left the house the nakodos take the couple to their bedroom, assist them to remove their garments and put them to bed. After they are well covered up another cup of saké is passed around and the final goodnights are repeated.

In the morning the father of the groom, or the nakodo, goes to police headquarters and registers the marriage, giving the names, ages, occupations and residence of the couple. It is customary for the bride and groom shortly after their marriage to make a present to the gentleman and lady who have served them as nakodos.

On the third day after the wedding the bride returns to her father's house to stay three or seven days, as the case may be, during which time her father invites the friends of both families—usually those who have been guests at the wedding—to a big feast. If the first three days of married life are not satisfactory to the bride, she notifies the nakodos of that fact and does not return to her husband's home, which is equivalent to a divorce. If the husband is dissatisfied he notifies the nakodos, and they are expected to communicate with the bride's parents. If a divorce is insisted upon by either party it must be accepted by the other, but such

Marriage and Divorce

a proceeding is seldom resorted to except where misrepresentations have been made as to the temper and physical condition of either party. If the bride or groom proves to be deformed, impotent or diseased in any manner a divorce is considered honorable and legitimate, and it is only necessary to register the fact at police headquarters.

After the ceremonies are concluded the bride separates herself entirely from her own family and becomes as much identified with the family of her husband as if she were born into it. She is not expected to inherit any of her father's property, although he may leave her a legacy if he desires to do so. Nor is it necessary for a father to give his daughter a dowry upon her marriage, although it is often done. It is usually a part of the original arrangement, and the amount is settled between her parents and the nakodos.

I asked one of the most progressive and modernized Japanese gentlemen I have ever met whether it were not possible for a young man to select his own bride and propose marriage to her or to her father according to the American plan. "Of course it is possible," he replied, "but it is extremely improbable. Our people are not educated up to that point. We may come to it in time, but marriage and the affairs of the home are the last to be affected by foreign

The Yankees of the East

innovations. .If a young man of the very highest reputation and social position should attempt to offer himself to a young lady, or ask her hand in marriage from her father, as you do in America, he would undoubtedly be kicked out of the house. It would be absolutely fatal to his prospects of marriage, for neither that girl nor any other girl with any self-respect would accept him. The result would be the same as if some some young man in America were to try the Japanese plan. He would be considered as trifling with the most sacred relation in life, and his friends would be advised to shut him up in a lunatic asylum. While our young people are not allowed to associate upon terms of intimacy with each other or even form friendships with unmarried persons of the opposite sex, they see each other frequently, so it is always possible, and often easy, for a young man to select his bride from among the families with which his parents are friendly. It is only necessary for him to notify his father or a nakodo of his wishes, and if the young lady is not otherwise provided for they can arrange matters to his satisfaction without the slightest difficulty."

In writing and speaking of Japan among the Japanese one has to be extremely careful in his references to the condition of women and to the subject of marriage and divorce. It is their weak point, and they are extremely sensitive

Marriage and Divorce

about it. The Rev. Mr. Tamura, pastor of one of the native Presbyterian churches in Tokyo, and one of the brightest and most energetic representatives of the Christian faith in Japan, was recently expelled from the presbytery for publishing a book in which the marriage relation and the enslavement of women were too freely discussed. It was entitled "The Japanese Bride," and was published in English for American readers.

Mr. Tamura had the usual author's allowance of ten copies sent him, which he presented, with his compliments, to prominent friends in and out of the church. They created a sensation—what Mr. Tamura himself calls a tempest—because no Japanese had ever discussed the subject so freely, or told the truth so plainly, or in cold type compared the condition of his mother and sister and wife with that of women in other lands. The book was taken up in the presbytery and the author was accused of slandering his people. He was not charged with falsehood, but with telling too much truth. It would not have been so bad, they argued, if the book had been written in Japanese for the purpose of encouraging a reform, but it was disgraceful for a clergyman to advertise the faults of his race among foreigners, for the purpose, as they claimed, of creating a sensation.

Mr. Tamura is, perhaps, best known in the

The Yankees of the East

United States of all the Japanese native preachers. He is a graduate of Princeton college and Auburn Theological seminary. He has occupied the pulpit of some Presbyterian church in nearly every city of size in America, and has made two lecturing tours for the purpose of raising money for an industrial school he established here some years ago. He has visited every state and territory except Texas, and his many friends in the United States will regret to learn of his trouble. But, although his fellow-Presbyterians punished him they did not quench his zeal nor injure his influence. When he was expelled from the presbytery his church went with him, and has since been more prosperous than before. The sympathies of the public, as is usual in such cases, are generally with him, and the missionary element of all denominations will only admit that he was guilty of an indiscretion.

There are no shrines or tablets erected to the memory of the good mothers and wives and daughters of Japan for the people to worship, although there are several goddesses, and one woman saint has crept into the Buddhist calendar. Her name is Chiu-Jo-Hime and she is commemorated with an idol. As near as I can ascertain her history, she was a nun, and they made her a saint because she discovered the usefulness of the fiber of the lotus root and wove it into tapestry for altar decoration. Ben-

Marriage and Divorce

ten is the goddess of good luck, and there are streets named after her in nearly all the cities. The principal shopping street in Yokohama is Benten-Dori. The next popular shopping street is Honchi-Dori, which means "a favorable location," and from it our familiar slang phrase, "hunky-dori" was probably derived. The deity who acts as regent of the Buddhist hell is Emma-O ; but he is a god.

Most of the goddesses are of evil disposition, and in the Japanese language there is no word to describe gallantry to women. In feudal times, when courage and skill in combat were the highest attributes of man, no Japanese knight ever performed a valiant deed for the love of a woman. He fought for the approval of his father or for the favor of his prince. Few Japanese poets and authors have written of love and woman's smiles. All of the poetry and literature that tends that way is not fit for maidens or missionaries to read. And it is not because woman is unworthy. Every one who has visited that country or has lived there will agree in their appreciation and their admiration of the virtues of the Japanese women, even if they are not unanimous as to their beauty. Judged by the artistic models, the classic faces and figures of Greece, or the types of beauty that we admire the most in the United States, the Japanese woman is not beautiful, but she is sweet and gentle and good. She suffers what few women are compelled to endure, but she never complains, and her influence in molding the character of her children and in shaping the civilization of this empire can never be overestimated.

But from birth a woman is taught that she is "the weaker vessel;" that she is an inferior being, created to minister to the will and the fancy of men. Her marriage is an affair with which she has nothing to do. Her husband is selected for her, and when he tires of her he can put her away.

There are seven causes, according to Confucius, for which a man may divorce his wife. They are disobedience, the failure to bear children, unchastity, jealousy, an incurable disease, dishonesty and a sharp tongue. In other words, he can get rid of her whenever he likes and by very simple process. All he has to do is to write her a letter declaring that everything is over between them, and advising her to return to her parents. Such a letter addressed to her father or her eldest brother, if she has no father, will answer the same purpose. Then he must go to the registrar's office and report himself as a divorced man.

A wife may get rid of her husband if she desires to do so for similar causes, but she will lose her social position, if she has any, and is much more likely to be respected and make a second

Marriage and Divorce

marriage if she is the defendant instead of the plaintiff in the case. This is somewhat of a paradox, but it throws a searchlight upon the social system of Japan. What is required above all from women is obedience. That is the highest of virtues, and no obedient woman would ever seek a divorce from her husband for any cause.

When a wife wishes to be divorced she writes a letter to her husband announcing that fact, packs up her things, notifies the registrar of vital statistics and goes back to her father's house. If there are children of immature years the couple dispose of them by agreement or by the arbitration of a mutual friend.

While divorces among the upper classes of Japan are very rare, it is doubtful if there is any country on earth where they are more frequent among the common people. I know the superintendent of the lighters of a steamship company at Yokohama who has been divorced nine times, and a missionary from Chicago told me that his former cook had had seven wives when he left the family four years ago, and that several had since been added to the list. The higher civilization advances in Japan the more numerous divorces appear to be. The following tables from the official records show the number of marriages and divorces each year in Japan since 1887, when the records became en-

The Yankees of the East

tirely reliable, and the percentage per 1,000 of population each year:

MARRIAGES.

YEAR	TOTAL NUMBER.	PER 1,000
1887	334,149	85.5
1888	330,246	83.4
1889	340,445	85.0
1890	325,141	80.4
1891	352,651	86.0
1892	349,489	85.8
1893	358,839	86.6

On December 31, 1894, there were 7,561,900 married couples in the empire of Japan, representing 367.88 out of every 1,000 of the population.

DIVORCES.

YEAR.	TOTAL NUMBER.	PER 1,000.
1887	110,859	28.4
1888	109,175	27.6
1889	107,458	26.8
1890	107,088	26.0
1891	112,411	27.6
1892	113,498	27.9
1893	116,775	28.2

It will thus be seen that the number of divorces taking place annually is about one-third as large as the number of marriages, and that the average runs about the same every year. It should be explained for the benefit of the incredulous, that these figures are taken from the Statistical Review of the Empire of Japan, published by order of the cabinet by the bureau of statistics at Tokyo.

The condensed returns do not show how many of these divorces were sought by husbands,

Marriage and Divorce

but I am informed by a gentleman who is familiar with the detailed returns that only about one per cent. originated with wives.

The morals of the women have very little to do with divorce. The prevailing cause is a lack of affection and dissatisfaction on the part of the men, who become tired of their wives and want to try another chance in the lottery of marriage. As a bad temper and incompatability are sufficient ground at any time for getting rid of a wife, a man does not hesitate long when he sees a woman he likes better than the one he is living with. The law of chastity applies to wives in Japan, but not to husbands. There is a double standard of morals prevailing from the nobility to the peasantry. The husband may be as licentious as he likes, and the wife seldom grumbles, for if she does she is liable to lose her home and be separated from her children; and, as she has been educated to believe that whatever man does is right, she doesn't think much about it.

A Japanese woman never addresses her husband in terms of endearment, nor has the Japanese man any pet names for his wife. While there is, no doubt, genuine affection and devotion on both sides in the large majority of families, both sexes have been taught to repress their emotions. A Japanese husband never kisses his wife or his children. He knows no

The Yankees of the East

such word as home. Children and wives are taught to respect and reverence the head of the family, be he father, husband, brother or son, and this deference is carried much further than with us; but if caresses are ever exchanged the world is not allowed to know it.

The husband introduces his wife to his friends with words ot depreciation. He says this is my "humble" wife, or my "stupid" wife, or my "unworthy" wife, or my "unfortunate" wife, just as he refers to his humble or unworthy home. The husband always precedes the wife whenever they enter a house or a room, or are walking together upon the streets. When guests are present the wife always takes a seat at a distance near the door. It is the duty of woman to wait upon man. If a mat, or tea, or anything else is wanted, the wife always goes for it. She is only a slight degree above the servants.

The Japanese say that this does not signify disrespect or a lack of affection, but it is the custom of the country, and that the women are as well satisfied with it as the men, but at the same time the educated Japanese always shrinks from a conversation on this subject.

The Japanese woman does not have a pretty figure. She is always short and stumpy. Her neck and waist are large, her shoulders are broad and her flesh seems to be evenly distributed. A modiste would say that she had no shape at all

Marriage and Divorce

and therefore it is impossible to make a modern dress fit her. The ancient style of garments. particularly those used by the upper classes, were especially adapted to the peculiarities of the Japanese women, and a lady always looks well in the soft grays and delicate tints that she selects for her kimonos. But one who will be very pretty and graceful in her native costume generally looks like a guy when she puts on a Paris dress, no matter how fine the material or who made it.

The modern costume is universally admired and it certainly adds to the dignity of a man. But as worn among the common people it certainly does not contribute to the grace or the modesty of the women, for it consists of a single garment fastened only with a girdle, which allows it to flop open both above and below the waist and expose a large portion of the person which women in other countries are taught to conceal. It should be said, however, that the Japanese women as a rule are very modest. A gentleman who has been living in Japan for more than a quarter of a century and has seen all there is in Japanese life, asserts that he never knew a native women to intentionally commit an impropriety.

But neither the Japanese lady nor gentleman is improved in appearance by modern dress. The men appear to have no idea of what looks

The Yankees of the East

well and wear the most outlandish combinations. You seldom see one clad in a full suit of the same color, and they do not like dark clothes. They usually have a blue coat, a pink vest, lavender trousers, a red necktie, a green hat, and if they can find a shirt of another color they put it on. In selecting their native costumes they choose quiet grays, blues and browns, and in the manufacture of fabrics and in the decorative arts no people are so skilfull in combining shades as the Japanese, but they do not seem to have the sense of good taste in the selection of European garments.

It is usually the case, too, that a young Japanese who puts on foreign garments thinks it necessary to adopt other foreign customs, and, not having a very clear idea as to what they are, makes a ridiculous spectacle of himself with the best of intentions. He puts his hat on the back of his head, sticks a cigar in the corner of his mouth, takes a cane in his hand, and thinks he is a perfect model of an American or an English gentleman, when in fact he is a poor imitation of a loafer. But I suppose that the Americans and Europeans who put on Japanese garments and attempt to imitate their manners are subject to the same criticisms. I heard a Japanese lady who had witnessed a performance of "The Mikado" in the United States, commenting upon the costumes in a very amusing way, and

THE NEW WAY.

Marriage and Divorce

from what she said I judge that, from the Japanese standpoint, the performers must have looked ridiculous.

The most interesting of all things Japanese are the children, and one sees them to the best advantage in the kindergartens, which are numerous throughout the country and are attached to all of the public schools, although many of them are very imperfect imitations of the genuine institutions that we have at home. The Japanese child is the father of the man, and when he is on parade or has anything serious before him he is the most dignified and decorous person in existence. When he is at play he is as happy as a child can be, and one of the most attractive scenes in Tokyo, Kyoto and other of the large cities are the play grounds around the schoolhouses at recess time.

As soon as a baby is born it is strapped on the back of an elder brother or sister with its little limbs closely confined and its head rolling about helplessly in the sun. It is a Japanese custom to shave the head of an infant on the seventh day after the birth, only a tiny tuft of hair on the nape of the neck being left, as a practical gentleman suggests, for seed. During the next five or six years, and often until the child is 10, the head is shaved at frequent intervals and in a most grotesque and absurd manner as the French shave the bodies of their

The Yankees of the East

poodle dogs. The spots that are made bare and those that are left unshaven indicate the taste of the tonsorial artist, and the poor little chaps are mutilated in such a way that, with their little black almond eyes, their serene and serious countenances and the gay kimonos in which they are dressed, it makes them look like the curious dolls you buy in the shops. This constant shaving of the head is the cause of the coarseness and stiffness of the Japanese hair.

Japanese children are well mannered from the cradle and both boys and girls are free from that awkwardness and shyness which affects European and American children. They are models of obedience also. A Japanese baby never cries and a Japanese child is seldom punished. They seem to be born with a respect for authority and a reverence for their parents which pervade the entire body politic and have permitted the same dynasty to govern Japan for 2,500 years.

The most successful kindergarten in Japan, one which is always pointed at as a model and visited by strangers, is in charge of Miss Annie L. Howe of Chicago. She has been in Japan for seven years and is regarded by both foreigners and officials as one of the most useful teachers the missionary boards have ever sent out. In connection with her kindergarten she has a training school for teachers, from which the best

Marriage and Divorce

instructors in the primary departments of the Japanese schools have come.

Every woman in Japan above the age of 15 years seems to own a baby and usually carries it around upon her back. They never cry—they never get impatient or discontented, but stay where they are put and enjoy it. You can see hundreds of women at work in the tea-firing houses, where the temperature is always very high and the work is very hard, going through their twelve hours of labor with babies 3 or 4 weeks old strapped upon their backs, and the babies never whimper no matter how much the mothers shake them when they are stirring the hot tea leaves with their arms up to their shoulders in the pans. Then, after three hours, when the regular resting time comes and everybody stops for refreshments, baby gets his. He is unstrapped and nursed while his mother is dipping into her little rice can with a couple of chopsticks, and then, when the whistle blows, he is strapped on again for another three hours, without opening his lips except to yawn or say "goo" or make some other remark as the events and peculiarities of this wonderful world excite his attention.

When he gets a little older his mother puts him in a tea box with some simple playthings, and he will stay there all day, safe from harm, and grow and enjoy himself. He can exercise

The Yankees of the East

his arms by pulling himself by the sides of the box, and his legs by treading around in that limited space, and can assist in the development of his dental apparatus by chewing the edges of the boards, but he never seems to get tired or hungry or dissatisfied, although any live American baby that ever existed would be howling like a drove of blue devils five minutes after his mother had gone to her work.

Toward noonday, when the sun gets hot and the little ones feel sleepy, they lie down on the floor like cats or dogs. It may be a pavement of brick or stone, it may be a board floor, but they need no cradle, or blanket, or pillow; only a sheltered corner out of the sun where they won't be stepped upon, and they do not have to be rocked or sung to sleep. They take care of themselves. Their mothers are busy earning 8, 10 and 15 cents a day by twelve or thirteen hours of hard labor in a warehouse where the temperature is often above 100 degrees all day long, and the odor of tea is so strong that it almost strangles you; so they do not think it fair to bother them or add to their cares, and have the good sense and self-control to find their own amusement and look after their own comfort, just like a puppy or a kitten.

That is the kind of baby they raise in Japan.

Mr. Daigoro Goh, an author and scholar of reputation, gives an interesting explanation of

THE OLD WAY.

Marriage and Divorce

the family relations in Japan, which is intended to counteract the effect of Mr. Tamura's "Japanese Bride."

"Whatever their religious faith may be," he says, "Japanese families carry out, informally, the teaching of morality in their own homes. The elders are the instructors of the younger, practicing as many rites of reverence and worship in the house as in the temple, every household, however humble, having a family ancestral altar and several domestic shrines of gods, where daily sacrifices and ceremonies are invariably performed, scrupulously preserving and adjusting the external proprieties of etiquette as well as the inner consciousness of juniors in the presence of seniors, pious devotion to the memory of ancestors, filial piety, loyalty, fraternal affection, faithfulness of husband and wife, respect to the old, kindness and sympathy to the young and weak, charity to the poor, and help to relations, being inculcated by the family teaching. In short, the ethics of the Japanese people are cultivated and kept up, in great measure, by domestic instruction.

"Among the relations of the Japanese family the first and foremost in importance is that between parents and children. Paternity on the one hand and filial piety on the other, are not only the tie between parent and child; they unite also the whole family. Good parents and

The Yankees of the East

dutiful children, according to the Japanese notion, are the makers of family unity and the factors of national peace and order. More importance is attached to this relationship in Japan than even to that between husband and wife. The latter relationship, the Japanese conceive, is a matter of mutual agreement, which can be dissolved by mutual consent; while the former, being a natural tie, cannot be annulled. The consequence is, to take an extreme case, that a husband can divorce his wife on the ground that his father and mother disagree so much with her as to cause constant family disturbance, but it is regarded, of course, as a most painful incident. Theoretically speaking, Japanese parents possess unlimited power over their children so long as this power is exerted for their benefit. On the other hand, Japanese youths are compelled by the national system of ethics, to pay the acknowledged duty of obedience to parents. Hence, it may be imagined, that Japanese children are far from enjoying happiness and liberty. Happily, however, Japanese fathers and mothers, as in other nationalities, have no lack of love or good will towards their children.

"Our forefathers used to propose directly to the girls whom they loved, without any go-between, who is indispensably employed for betrothing by the existing people. The bridegroom, in that simple and happy era, instead of

Marriage and Divorce

holding the wedding ceremony at the paternal house, whither the bride of the present time has to go first for the wedding, had to betake himself to the bride's paternal home to celebrate the union, and, staying there a night, take back the new wife to his own house the following day. At this ceremony the wedding wine was drunk first by the bride, and the cup offered afterwards to the bridegroom, which etiquette is entirely opposed to the present practice. The two customs last named, I am informed, are in practice at the present day in certain localities of our ancient empire. These usages seemed to have lasted only up to the ninth century of the Christian era, when Chinese influence commenced to remodel the whole framework of social life, and the original initiative of the country, in consequence, gradually lost ground.

"From the seventh to the fifteenth century of the Christian era, so preponderant was Chinese influence over the court, laws, science, art, and literature, that even the status of woman was copied from the Celestial empire, where the fair sex is considered impure in its physical formation, defective in its mental constitution, and consequently inferior in its position, both domestic and social.

"This peaceful but evolutionary era was followed by the 'Belligerent Age,' which lasted till the establishment of the Tokugawa feudalism

The Yankees of the East

three centuries ago. This disorderly 'Middle Age' struck another blow at the weaker sex. The intellectual progress was sadly impaired, the civil administration was neglected in a most lamentable manner; military exploits, physical strength, valiant deeds, and adventure were the sole admiration and ambition of the time. At such a period it is but natural that the stronger sex should have ascendency in every way over the weaker, a state which may be easily vouched for by the history of Europe. Moreover, the science and literature of the time were left almost exclusively in the hands of the Buddhist priest, the only ruler of the intellectual and moral world of the age, and who was also another foe to woman. The Buddhist creed in this respect is no better than the Chinese philosophy. 'Woman has no home in the three worlds—past, present and future' ('Sangai ni iye nashi')—is one of their popular precepts, and thus every right of the fair sex was violated.

"The next stage was the Tokugawa period. Peace was restored, art and science were recovered and promoted, social order gradually resumed its normal condition. But again, the mania for Chinese assimilation and politics, in social life, in science, and above all, in morality, having risen higher than ever, woman's position had sunk deeper and deeper in the social stratum.

Marriage and Divorce

"This is a historical epitome of the causes of the inferior position occupied by women in Japan. If, therefore, Japan had been free from external influence, the condition of the present woman, I am convinced, might have been quite different from what we now witness. Whatever the causes may have been it is my duty to present a faithful picture of the existing state of married life and to point out its defects as well as its virtues for the consideration of the Japan of the future.

"First of all the fundamental principle of marriage in Japan must be clearly understood before we proceed further. Marriage, to speak strictly in our national sense, is not merely for love but to constitute a family in order to secure the succession of a man's house established by his progenitor.

"Although I am myself an uncompromising opponent, up to a certain point, of the old system of married life, it is only just that I should as an exponent of the subject, desire to defend the Japanese husband, in the first place, against the undiscriminating attacks made by outsiders, since I have found there are some reasonable causes, historical, traditional, political and social for the supremacy given to the husband over the wife, and which is not exclusively due to motives of selfishness and oppression on the part of the stronger, as some critics allege. It is the man's

The Yankees of the East

house for which the benefit of marriage is intended, it is the man's family for which posterity is to be secured, it is the man's house in which the wife has to live and make her home; and, above all, it is the husband who has the entire responsibility of the maintenance of his wife and family. Moreover, the husband is, in general, the head of a family, and the sole possessor of the property. One more cause, which has been an essential factor, is the traditional belief of the people, emphasized, if not entirely taught, by the heresy of Confucius and Buddhism, as to the natural superiority, both mental and physical, of the stronger sex over the weaker. Putting together these facts and causes, we are able fairly to come to the conclusion that it has been not unreasonable for the Japanese husband to occupy, in practice as well as in principle, a higher level than that afforded to his wife. In other words, the Japanese conjugal life is not of the nature of a joint stock company, if I may be allowed to use this commercial metaphor, but that of a private firm owned by a certain person who has a junior partner to co-operate in business, the former retaining still the sole power and influence over the whole concern.

"What is only objectionable in the Japanese married life, however, has been, and still is, I am afraid, the abuse of this liberty and right of the husband, and, still worse, recognizing the abuses

Marriage and Divorce

as a matter of course. Unfortunately, the inequality of the Japanese husband and wife in their rights and liberties is rather excessive. Every restriction is imposed on her. Every submission is expected from her. She has to wait upon him at meals in the absence of servants. She has to salute him first on every occasion, and he merely returns her salutation. She walks, sits, eats, sleeps, all after him, and rises before him in the morning. She has to sit up and wait until any hour, in principle, but up to a reasonable time in practice, when he is out. She addresses him as Danna Sama, or "My Lord;" whereas he calls her by name. If any friend of the husband calls, while he is conversing with the visitor in the drawing room, the wife, in the next room, has to attend to, or superintend a servant in serving the guest with futon, or cushion, Tabako-bon, or smoking-tray, Hibachi, or fire-box, tea, and cake; but she seldom joins in the conversation unless the visitor be a lady. Housekeeping is her sole duty and responsibility, governing and directing the whole of the household affairs; but this is done rather for the benefit of the husband than for herself. In arranging rooms, preparing meals, employing servants, shopping, all his ideas, his tastes, his will, his requirements, are thought of first by the wife.

"The subordination of the wife to the husband cannot be perfected by one day's training. From her early childhood the girl is trained up in one direction only, that of obedience and faithfulness, as, in Japan every girl is supposed to be destined to be married.

"Miss Bacon recognizes, in her admirable book entitled 'Japanese Girls and Women,' that 'the Japanese woman is, under this discipline, a finished product at the age of sixteen or eighteen. She is kind, sweet and amiable, with greater power of self-control, and a knowledge of what is right to do upon all occasions.' If this perfection be the result of the restrictive measures applied in her training, why should not we adopt similar measures with the husband as well? I suggest, therefore, instead of the emancipation of women that the repression of men may be the preferable measure for Japan.

"No Japanese woman, however wealthy at her birth, brings any dowry to her husband's house at her marriage other than her wedding trousseau. This is simply because she comes to live under the roof of the husband's house, and makes no independent home for herself. Hence her life is entirely dependent upon her husband, and, at the same time, if any man marry a girl on condition of her bringing a dowry, he is considered morally mean and unmanly.

"Like marriage, divorce in Japan is entirely conducted by the family tribunal, and no judi-

Marriage and Divorce

cial proceedings are required for it. The only legal forms in the matter are the two following : The husband gives to the disunited wife Ri Yen Fo, or the letter of divorcement, which invariably consists of only three lines and a half of writing. Hence the phrase ' Mi kudari han,' or the 'three lines and a half,' became the representative term of divorce. No superstitious person would write an ordinary letter the same length as that of that unlucky document. The second necessary formality is to report the unfortunate event to the local registrar's office, and remove the name of the discarded wife from the registered membership of the husband's family. These two steps, in theory, suffice to sever the sacred union. Hence, one might infer the Japanese divorce to be as easy in practice as in its formal proceedings. But the actual state of the matter is very different from the supposition.

"Although the Japanese divorce requires no such elaborate public proceedings as in England, it is never settled by the parties themselves, except perhaps among the lowest classes, who may separate as easily as they unite. The reasons of the disagreement between the parties must first of all be submitted to the parents and the Nakadochi (the go-betweens), who try their best to allay the conflict, and advise the

The Yankees of the East

parties not to take such a scandalous course; if this preliminary pacification should not be successful, then the case may be brought before the other relatives of the husband and wife. At this family conference the case may be thoroughly examined, and the consequences of the separation fully discussed with prudence and justice, and the final decision may be given to the effect either of reunion or separation.

"It is also generally said that owing to its simple and easy process, there is statistically an alarming number of divorces in Japan. This assertion also needs a little rectification. The cases of so-called Ri yen may be more numerous in Japan than so-called divorces in England; but one point must not be forgotten, that there are no such practices in Japan as judicial separation and private separation, which may number as many if not more than the divorces. Reformation on these points is one of the immediate needs of the nation. Happily, the forthcoming civil code is expected to aim at bringing this customary usage into closer conformity with European ideas in this respect. The present government, fully recognizing the unquestionable necessity of reconstituting and reforming both the family and social organizations in conformity with the demands of the progressive age, and for the advancement of

Marriage and Divorce

the national welfare and prosperity, began more than ten years ago the responsible work of the codification of the civil and commercial laws, with the invaluable assistance of several eminent jurists of England, Germany, America and particularly France."

X
Japanese Journalism

The Japanese are well supplied with newspapers in their own language. When modern institutions were introduced into Japan and popular suffrage elected a parliament, journalism came with a rush, and it seemed as if almost everybody who was possessed of a political ambition and a sufficient sum of money to buy type and presses started an organ to proclaim his views to the people. Many of these endeavors were short lived, and monthly, weekly and daily publications rose and fell for five or six years like toadstools in the forest. The survival of the fittest has left Japan with a superabundance of political journals and a sufficient number of other periodicals devoted to literature, science and art.

There are nearly 600 newspapers in the empire and seventeen or eighteen political dailies in the city of Tokyo alone, which represent the several factions into which suffrage has divided the people. The subscription lists of some are decidedly small and are limited to the personal and political adherents of the editor or the

Japanese Journalism

leader in whose interest it is published. Such publications have their largest circulation through copies distributed free for the purpose of affecting public opinion.

The papers with the largest subscription lists are those which support the government, and are edited under the direction of the ministry. One of them, the Asahi Shimpo, which is published simultaneously at Osaka and Tokyo, is said to have a circulation of 300,000 daily, and is edited with great ability and truly American enterprise. The name in English means Rising Sun (Asahi), News Announcement (Shimpo). There are several with a circulation of 20,000 or more each, representing different political parties, but 10,000 or 15,000 copies is considered a profitable patronage.

The cost of running a paper in Japan is very low, as the best printers and pressmen do not receive half as much wages as the 'prentice boys in the United States. The foreman of the composing-room of the wealthiest newspaper in Japan is paid about as much as the boy who brings dispatches from the telegraph office to the editorial room in our country. But the subscription and advertising rates are nearly as high as those ordinarily charged with us. The average daily sells on the street for five sen, which is equal to two and a half cents in gold, and the best ones bring ten sen, which is equal

The Yankees of the East

to five cents in our money. Regular subscribers are served for from twenty-five to fifty cents (gold) a month, and the price per year varies from $6 to $10 (gold).

The number of attaches connected with the Japanese newspapers is large, but their compensation is correspondingly small. A good reporter would be glad to get a salary of five dollars a week, while a managing editor would be perfectly satisfied with $12 or $13. Some of the reporters are paid as low as two dollars a week, and political writers and other members of the editorial staff generally receive from four dollars to ten dollars a week, according to their ability and reputation.

The editor-in-chief, or the director, as he is called, is generally a politician, a man who has been or hopes to be a member of parliament or a cabinet minister, and the ardor with which his paper attacks or sustains a party in power usually indicates his opinion of his own prospects.

Mr. Fukuzawa, the editor of Jiji Shimpo, the leading independent paper of Tokyo, and in some respects the ablest journal in the East, is perhaps the most remarkable man in Japan. He is called "The Great Commoner," and is usually compared to John Bright, but is more like Horace Greeley. He is both an editor and schoolmaster by trade.

Japanese Journalism

The Keio Gijiku, a college of which he is the owner and president, is the most famous private institution in the land, and was the first of the native schools to adopt the modern foreign system of education. He has about 1,500 young men under his immediate charge studying the sciences, law, medicine, engineering, political economy, art, music and other branches of learning, and his vigorous personality pervades the entire institution. He teaches no special line of studies himself, but occupies a unique position. He lives in the school, associates intimately with the boys, treats them as if they were his own sons, assumes a general direction of matters of amusement, discipline and study, and is likely to drop into a class-room at any time and deliver a lecture to the students on the lesson of the day or on any other subject that may enter his mind. Every week or so he assembles the students in the lecture-room and talks to them for an hour or two on politics, history, morals or the topic which is uppermost in his thoughts at that particular time. He is a powerful orator, without a superior and with few equals in Japan, and when the spirit moves him he often hires a hall and delivers a public address on a political issue or any other idea that may be occupying the minds of the people.

Unselfish, eccentric, original, eloquent, sincere and patriotic, whether in the editorial chair,

The Yankees of the East

upon the lecture platform or in his school, Mr. Fukuzawa is undoubtedly the most influential private citizen in the empire. He has repeatedly refused office, although three times invited to a place in the ministry, and a dozen times or more proposed as a candidate for parliament, and has even rejected a title of nobility and several decorations that have been offered him by the emperor. When the present cabinet was formed he was slated as minister of education, but refused that honor as he has refused all others, because, as he told me, he did not want his hands to be tied. He prefers to stay outside the government, where he can throw stones. He belongs to no particular political party, but is thoroughly independent, and is supporting and opposing the government by turns, as it happens to meet his approval or disapproval. He is not always consistent, and declares that it is an evidence of sincerity when a man changes his mind. He has always been an earnest advocate of the introduction of foreign methods and modern ideas into Japan, is an apostle of religious tolerance, and, although professing no religion himself, declares that Christianity is the handmaid of civilization, and the education of the common people is the only method of perpetuating good government.

Mr. Fukuzawa's sons have the actual editorial and business management of his paper, but it

Japanese Journalism

seldom appears without an editorial from his vigorous pen; and he always writes it before breakfast. Like Horace Greeiey, he is an early riser, and when the larks are singing their morning hymn in the groves of Azabu he is sitting at his desk denouncing some great wrong or advocating some great reform with an ardor and emphasis that are peculiarly his own. Then when the last line of copy is finished Mr. Fukuzawa goes to a shed behind his stables and pounds rice for an hour or so—which is his daily exercise—just as the great American editor used to chop wood.

The existence of a bureau of censorship has a tendency to moderate the expression of views on the part of the opposition papers. When I arrived in Japan in May, 1895, shortly after the ratification of the treaty of peace and the surrender of the Liao Tung peninsula, eleven of the seventeen dailies in Tokyo had suspended publication at the request of the police because of indiscreet comments concerning the policy of the government.

The system is different there from that in other countries. In Europe a publisher is required to submit proof sheets of the matter he intends to publish to an agent of the bureau of censorship, who occupies a desk in his office, and when the latter places the word "forbidden" with a rubber stamp upon the face of a

The Yankees of the East

proof the type is sent to the dead galley. In Japan a newspaper is allowed to print whatever it pleases, and is afterward punished by the police if its articles or news are offensive. It may be temporarily or permanently suppressed. The publisher may be fined or imprisoned, or both, but his property cannot be confiscated without a hearing in court. The imprisonment is little better than a farce. As some papers in the United States are supposed to maintain a fighting editor, so in Japan there is a jail editor connected with every establishment which tends toward an unlawful freedom of speech. When the police call around at the office and ask for the responsible editor they are referred to this gentleman, who is calmly marched off to jail and serves a term of imprisonment to atone for an offense he is known not to have committed. His employer, who actually wrote or directed the writing of the offensive publication, in the meantime continues to occupy his seat in parliament and tiffin at his club. Everybody knows that the man in jail is a scapegoat, and that he is employed solely for that purpose.

There are four English dailies published in Yokohama and three more in other parts of the empire. There is one weekly society paper edited by an American. It is called the "Box of Curios," and was originally an advertising medium for dealers in bric-à-brac for free dis-

Japanese Journalism

tribution among the tourist hotels, but it was so successful that the editor enlarged it and charged a subscription fee. It is bright and entertaining and given to personalities and gossip about the members of the foreign colony and distinguished visitors, who buy copies to send to their friends at home.

The other papers are edited by British subjects, and are devoted to British interests. The Japanese Mail, the most important and widely circulated, receives an indirect subsidy from the Japanese government in the form of a permanent subscription for several thousand copies, and is intended to keep the foreign newspapers properly informed as to political affairs in the empire. Its editor, Captain Brinkley, is a retired British army officer, who has lived many years in Japan, has a Japanese wife, speaks, reads and writes the language fluently, and is considered the best authority on Japanese art among the foreign residents. He has the confidence of the ministry as well as the public, and exercises considerable influence personally as well as through his paper.

The other English papers are more or less opposed to the policy of the government, and carry on spirited debates with the editor of the Mail. Some of them, no doubt, intend to be fair and impartial, but others are inclined to spitefulness and print what the Japanese papers

The Yankees of the East

are not permitted to publish. Their circulation is limited. The subscription price is $1 a month, and single copies are sold for 20 sen (10 cents). The weekly editions, which contain summaries of the news and leading editorials, are $14 a year and 50 sen (25 cents) a number. Their advertising patronage, which comes from the steamship companies and foreign tradesmen, enables them to live. None of them take cable dispatches, but depend entirely upon the Japanese journals for their news.

Their devotion to British commercial interests in Japan is consistent and commendable, and they exercise considerable influence upon trade. They are equally consistent in their hostility to everything that is American, and never lose an opportunity to depreciate and discourage all that concerns the interests of the United States. This is recognized by the public and the officials of the government, and therefore it does comparatively little harm, but constant hammering cannot but leave an impression, and there ought to be some newspaper in Japan devoted to American interests. The manufacturers of the United States could well afford to pay the expense of a publication for the purpose of bringing their merchandise to the attention of the Japanese, and keeping the people informed as to the progress of events in America. I was assured by a prominent official of the Japanese government

THE NEW-FASHIONED WAY OF SPINNING.
COTTON FACTORY, OSAKA.

Japanese Journalism

that a liberal subsidy, similar to that given the Mail, would be paid to assist in sustaining a reputable and well-edited American newspaper for its usefulness in keeping Japanese affairs properly before the American people.

The British also enjoy a decided advantage over Americans in the matter of trade in Japan in the simple fact that they advertise their interests. Their manufacturers publish catalogues in the Japanese language with detailed descriptions of their goods and illustrations that are at once attractive and informing. I found dozens of catalogues of British firms published in the native language, but not one from any institution in America. Johnny Bull is very much more enterprising than Uncle Sam in this respect. He realizes the value of such agencies in extending his foreign trade. England has the lion's share of the imports of the Japanese market because she has made such intelligent efforts to place her goods. The representatives of her export interests are always on the lookout for opportunities to benefit themselves, and use them promptly and intelligently.

Another important matter which cannot be too strongly urged upon the attention of those whom it may concern, is the entire absence of telegraphic news from America in the Japanese papers. They have plenty of trivial information, from England chiefly, and from other parts of

The Yankees of the East

Europe to a limited degree, but one who reads nothing but their own news columns would never know that there was such a place as the United States. For at least three months in 1895 I took notes of the telegraphic news in the Japanese papers, and the only dispatch from the United States was under a London date and read as follows:

"A free-silver convention has been held at Memphis (U. S.). Two thousand one hundred of the delegates present advocated the rehabilitation of silver at the ratio of 16 to 1."

There was no reference in the cable news service to the death of Secretary Gresham nor to the appointment of Mr. Olney as his successor. Brief announcements of both events were furnished the press at Tokyo by the American minister. At the same time we had detailed information as to the movements of the Bedouins at Jiddah, the entertainments that were offered Shazada Nazrullah, the second son of the ameer of Afghanistan, in London, full accounts of cricket matches played at Gloucester and Middlesex, and were advised by cable that Mr. Grace, who made 169 runs, received a great ovation and a letter of congratulation from the prince of Wales and that a national cricket testimonial had been proposed for his benefit.

Reuter's agency informed us fully concerning the parliamentary election in England; that

Japanese Journalism

Mr. W. Saunders, liberal, from Walworth, would not be a candidate again, and that Mr. B. F. Williams, the unionist candidate for West Dorset was likely to be elected by an increased majority. We had excellent reports of the debate over the right of a peer to sit in the house of commons, and abstracts of speeches by Sir William Vernon Harcourt at a banquet in Liverpool, where he asserted that there was a great depression in England, notably in agriculture, but some signs of improvement. We learned all about Oscar Wilde's trial, and the circumstances under which Arthur Orton, the Tichborne claimant, confessed himself a fraud. We kept track of Lord Rosebery on his yachting tour, and knew that Adelina Patti would entertain the duke and duchess of York. The sale of the jewels of the duchess of Montrose was fully reported, as was the trial of Jabez Balfour in the Bow street police court. We were informed regularly concerning the opinion of the London Times on the various public questions of the day, and had a long dispatch about a proposition to give extra pay to the British troops in Chitral, but stirring events in our own country were never referred to.

From France the news was not so profuse, but similar. For example, we learned by cable that a woman named Amelot, a "folle mystique," assassinated the Abbe de Broglie, brother of the Duc de Broglie; that a military school of medicine was to be established at Lyons; that Gen. Zurlindere had publicly reaffirmed his belief in the soundness of the French military system; that M. Ribot had submitted the annual budget to the chamber of deputies with various details thereof, and we had an excellent account of the robbery of a railway office in the interior of France by means of false keys.

Cablegrams of a similar nature are received daily by the Japanese papers from Germany, Italy and Austria, and now and then something from Belgium and other European countries, but never a word from the United States. All this has its effect in keeping up an association between the Japanese and the countries of Europe, and the absence of intelligence from the United States naturally suggests that the great American republic is of too little importance to deserve public notice. All of the news agencies that serve the papers are under British influence and control, and it is their policy to ignore the United States so far as possible.

The founder of Japanese journalism was an Englishman, Mr. John Black, one of the earliest foreign residents of Yokohama. There were periodicals printed before the restoration, but they were purely literary, and contained poems, stories, historical articles, political essays, narratives of travel and other contributions and facts of general interest, but nothing like news. And some of the job printers were in the habit of printing from wooden blocks small bulletins whenever some horrible murder or disaster or other sensational event took place. They were brief and irregular, and were not delivered to subscribers, but only sold on the street. Sometimes men who had exclusive information of such a kind would write it out themselves or hire some literary man to write it for them, then take the manuscript to a job printing office and have so many hundred or thousand copies "struck off," which they would sell for their own profit by sending carriers through the streets.

It was not until 1871 that anything resembling a newspaper was issued. Then appeared a political pamphlet somewhat resembling the modern American railway folder, which was published at regular intervals in the interest of Kido, a prominent politician. It was called the Zasshi-Shimbun, or, "the political newspaper." The Nasshin-Shinjishi, started by Mr. Black in 1872, was, however, the first journalistic venture devoted to news and dependent upon the public for support. Then, as the spirit of enterprise developed, the empire was overwhelmed with a multitude of newspapers. Within a few years more than six hundred were published in various cities of the country. The contents of most of them were limited to editorial discussion of public questions, and represented the views of ambitious

The Yankees of the East

politicians. But as the same laws apply to newspapers as to natural history, the weak ones died and the strong ones were preserved to exert an influence upon the social and political revolution that regenerated Japan, perhaps more extensive than the editorial profession have ever exercised in any other country.

It is said that the Buddhist priests brought the art of printing into Japan from China, and it is probably true. The earliest example of printing extant are Buddhist charms and amulets which the Empress Shotoku caused to be distributed among the temples in the year 770. You can see these ancient slips in the museums. The oldest printed book known in Japan was produced in 1198. The Precepts of Confucius were printed in 1364. The first work of importance to appear in print was the Nihongi, which contains the mythology and early history of the empire, said to have been composed in 720, but the earliest existing editions are dated 1599. A collection of poems entitled "Manyoshu," dating from the middle of the eighth century was also printed about the same time. All of these books were reproduced from engraved blocks. Metallic type were not introduced into Japan until 1870, and block printing is not entirely abandoned. You still find it used in the country towns, and the Peking Gazette, the official organ of the Chinese government, and the oldest

Japanese Journalism

newspaper in the world, is yet printed daily from engraved blocks in the same form and style in which it has appeared for more than eight hundred years. It is a little pamphlet of twenty-four pages, about three by nine inches in size, with leaves of very thin rice paper, and a cover of yellow—the imperial color—of a little heavier weight. The cover bears an ancient title, and the seal or imprint of the printer. The last page is the first, and you read from right to left instead of from left to right as with us. The first paragraphs in the book are court announcements. Then come the imperial decrees, then the full text or abstracts of memorials that have been submitted to the emperor, and have been or are being considered, and finally such announcements of future events as are considered important to the public.

A Japanese editor writes with a long brush similar to, but a little larger than, a camel's hair pencil, which he dips into ink that he makes as he needs it. The Japanese writing apparatus is lacquer tray with a little compartment for brushes of different sizes, a tiny jar of water, a cake of what we call India ink, and a little porcelain tablet with a shallow reservoir in the top. Before commencing a letter or an article the editor moistens the cake of ink in the jar of water and rubs it upon the porcelain. This leaves a sediment of intense black, which is

The Yankees of the East

diluted to the proper consistency by dipping the brush into the water and stirring it again. His stationery is a roll of paper six or eight inches wide, and his brush moves from right to left instead of from left to right, as with us.

All the government engraving, lithographing and printing, including the manufacture of bank bills and postage and revenue stamps in Japan is done at an institution known by the simple and expressive name of Insetsukioku. It occupies a fine building of French architecture, recently erected and equipped with all the improvements and conveniences of a well-ordered printing office, whose capacity is insufficient and the increasing business has caused an overflow into a number of ancient and ill-arranged structures that have long occupied the densely shaded grounds that were once the abode of a prince. The employes wear uniforms of white cotton while at work, which are changed for their ordinary street dress when they leave the building. Many, perhaps two-thirds of them, are women and girls, who look very neat and orderly in their scanty raiment, for it is but a single garment, without buttons, only held together by a girdle around the waist, and discloses a considerable portion of their person, which in other countries it is considered modest to conceal. But their unconscious innocence feels no shame.

Upon the left arm of each employe is a series

of short stripes of red, which indicate rank and length of service. Some of them have four, five and six stripes, showing that they are veterans. The foremen or forewomen of the several divisions have another distinctive badge.

The machinery is mostly of French and German manufacture. Much of it was made in Japan upon stolen patents, for the government has only to buy one press or piece of apparatus. The ingenious machinists of the country will produce as many copies as are needed without eompunction or lack of skill, although Japanese imitations are not always as durable as the models. I could only find one machine from the United States, and that was a big trimming knife in the bindery. The secretary and assistant superintendent, who showed us around, said that there was no objection to American machinery. They agreed that the best presses in the world were made in the United States, but the institution was organized and equipped by Europeans under contract, and they naturally preferred what they were familiar with.

The government makes its own inks, type and other supplies, and has a mill in the suburbs of Tokyo at which every grade, from the finest bond to ordinary printing paper, is manufactured. The Japanese, as we all know, make the best papers in the world. There are machine shops connected with the Insetsukioku, at which

The Yankees of the East

all repairs are made and conventional machinery, and nothing is bought abroad except an occasional press or some recent improvement, which, as I have said, is immediately imitated.

The natives make excellent engravers, and have the highest degree of artistic skill and taste. Some of the designers are eminent artists, and samples of their work which were displayed in an exhibition-room surpassed anything I have ever seen in France or Germany. But their wages are absurdly low. The highest salary paid among the engravers and artists is equivalent to only $45 a month in our money, and this commands their entire time and talent. The superintendent of the institution, who ranks next to a member of the cabinet, gets about the same pay as the messenger in the government printing office at Washington. The lowest wages paid among the 600 employes, is five sen, or two and a half cents a day to the young girls who carry the printed sheets from the presses to the drying-rooms, and hang them over the wires. The average is twenty-four sen, or twelve cents a day in our money, and this for eleven hours work—from seven in the morning till six at night, with half an hour's rest at noon for luncheon.

The composing room of a Japanese printing office would appall an American printer. The ordinary Japanese vocabulary is represented by

Japanese Journalism

4,427 different characters or ideographs and forty-seven simple characters, known as kana, which are used to connect and complete them. For official business, such as the printing required by the executive departments of the government, 2,506 more characters are needed, and to set the parliamentary debates 5,987 more are necessary, making a total of 10,920 different characters in a single font, such as is used in the Insetsukioku. Nor is that the limit. There are between 14,000 and 20,000 more ideographs in the scientific vocabulary, and I was told that it would require at least 80,000 varieties of letters to answer all possible demands of Japanese published literature. Think of a printer's case containing 80,000 compartments.

The government is endeavoring to simplify the Japanese vocabulary and reduce it to reasonable limits. A commission of scholars and philologists was appointed some time ago by the minister of education upon the recommendation of a national teachers' convention, and they are said to be making some progress, although their task is a most difficult one. There is no alphabet of the Japanese language, as we understand that term. Each word is represented by a different character or ideograph, whose meaning is modified or enlarged by the addition of a kana as necessary, used either as a prefix or suffix, or both.

The Yankees of the East

A font of Japanese type occupies a space about twelve or fifteen feet square. It is a pen of racks and cases, arrayed in the form of a hollow square, with a narrow passage to afford an entrance and exit. The chief compositor sits at a table in the center with a case containing a supply of the forty-seven kana before him and a long peculiar-looking composing stick in his hand. He cuts his copy into small "takes" and gives one to each of his five or six assistants, who are usually small boys and girls with astonishing memories. With their "takes" held deftly with their composing sticks in their left hands, they rush around and pick the type that are needed from the bewildering mass of cases, singing aloud the name of the character until they find it. The work of composition is, therefore, a bedlam, which would drive an American printer out of his wits.

The uneducated Japanese cannot recognize the meaning of a printed character by the eye, but only by the ear. Therefore he must read aloud. The common people always have to read their newspapers aloud to understand them. Formerly all the children studied aloud, and a traveler always knew when he was in the neighborhood of a school by the sound of their voices, the same as a sawmill or a boiler factory; but the government has prohibited this in the public schools, and the youngsters are taught by sight

Japanese Journalism

and not by sound in these days of modern innovations. But in the interior you still find the old-fashioned method of learning in use.

When a boy has collected all the characters in his "take" he places the composing stick with the copy upon the table before the chief compositor, who wears a big pair of strong magnifying glasses, and he arranges them in his own stick in their proper order, inserting the kana from his own case where they are needed. Then he dumps them on a galley and turns them over to the proper attendant, who pulls a proof and takes it to the proof-reader, who reads it aloud while his assistant holds the copy and follows him.

It is explained that children are used to assist the compositor because they have better memories than adults, and their little fingers are more deft in picking the type out of the narrow little slips. The extraordinary memory of a child compositor is always amazing to the stranger in Japan. But the race has been trained by the experience of centuries to remember. A Japanese never forgets anything. And when you realize that all education is a simple matter of memory the phenomenon is not so strange. Every word in the language is represented by a different character, and, as I have said, there are over four thousand words in the ordinary conversational vocabulary. The vocabulary of

The Yankees of the East

the peasant class is, of course, much more limited and contains perhaps seven hundred or eight hundred words. But to read an ordinary, simple book one must be able to recognize at least two thousand signs.

The child in the primary school begins by learning simple sentences, and commits to memory every word sign in his primer. Then he takes a higher step, a wider range of words, as he advances into literature, until, when he has reached the grammar school, his little mind is stored with an enormous number of words, and is able to identify the signs that represent them and the meaning they are intended to convey.

A case of type is about three feet long and two feet wide, divided into two grand divisions by a horizontal partition. Then each division is subdivided into equal little narrow slips just wide enough to admit the type, which are all of the same size, and stand on end with their faces upward. This simple illustration will convey a clearer idea than a verbal description :

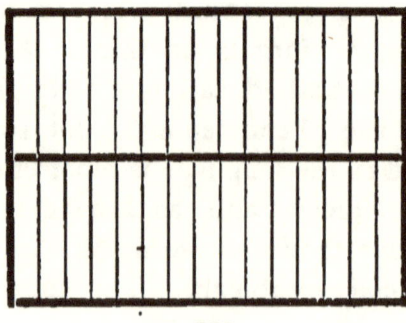

Japanese Journalism

There are usually forty slips in each division and eighty in each case. The cases are usually double, and therefore contain 160 different characters. On each rack are twelve cases and 1,920 kinds of type. So that twelve racks will carry a very full font of type, containing about 23,000 characters, sufficient to supply almost any demand. The ordinary composing room contains about six racks, or 10,000 varieties of type, with plenty of room for sorts.

The Japanese language was imported from China, and was originally a combination of pictographs. The original word for tree was a rude picture of that object, and has been reduced and simplified by usage until it is now a fixed sign. Each nation has made modifications, but has built its own language upon the same fundamental principles. Many of the same signs are still preserved in both languages, and it is said that a Japanese can read Chinese easier than a Chinaman can read Japanese. But in both countries the spoken language is very different from the written language, and many people who can read newspapers cannot read books, because the vocabulary of the former is simpler and more limited. People of literary accomplishments use terms that never appear in the newspapers and are not heard in conversation.

Missionaries who can preach in Japanese fluently and can read the bible are often unable

The Yankees of the East

to read ordinary books, for the language of the scriptures differs widely from that used by modern writers. There are many missionaries in Japan who have never been able to conquer the literary language of the country because they lack the power of memory that the natives have inherited, and, although they may be able to converse readily, they must have their dictionaries beside them if they attempt to read a letter or a newspaper.

XI
Concerning Trade and Investments

Mr. Dun, the United States minister at Tokyo, told me that in his opinion the outlook for commercial and industrial enterprises was brighter in Japan than in any other part of the world—that there was no more profitable field for investment. Mr. Dun has lived in Japan almost continuously for twenty-three years and knows the country and the people. He went there in 1872 with General Horace Capron, who had been commissioner of agriculture at Washington, for the purpose of organizing an agricultural department and establishing an experimental farm for the Japanese government. A number of other young men from the civil service at Washington were employed at the same time to assist in modernizing the executive branches of the government. He has been a member of the United States legation for several years and was appointed minister by Mr. Cleveland at the beginning of his second administration.

Mr. Dun says that almost every kind of manufacturing pays in Japan, and there is an open-

The Yankees of the East

ing for almost every sort of factory. Labor is so cheap and so skillful, fuel is so cheap, and there is a growing demand for all the myriad articles that enter into the wants of civilized men. Manufacturing has been conducted in the households of Japan until very recently. Every man did his work under his own roof, assisted by his wife and children, and the latter usually followed the trade of their parents. Factories were unknown, and they are very few in number even now, although they are increasing rapidly.

The success of a manufacturing enterprise in Japan, Mr. Dun says, is entirely a matter of management. Investments are as safe there as anywhere else in the world, although there is comparatively little foreign capital represented. All the railroads, which now represent a total of about 3,000 miles and an investment of $75,000,000, were built with local capital. Not a dollar was borrowed abroad, and there are very few shares or bonds of Japanese corporations held by foreign investors. At the same time the people are not rich. There are very few men of large fortunes. I was told by a Tokyo banker that he knew of but two millionaires in Japan. One made his money in coal-mining and the other is the principal owner of the Nippon Yusen Kaisha, the great steamship company which has nearly 100 vessels in its service and a

Concerning Trade and Investments

monopoly of the coasting trade. But there are many men with small fortunes, and although wages are very low, nobody is very poor. I did not hear of an almshouse in the entire empire, and I seldom saw a beggar on the street. Occasionally some poor leper stretches out his hand as you enter one of the gilded temples, but there isn't a country in Europe or America so free from street begging.

The people as a rule are frugal, economical and manage to save a little even when they are working for 10 cents a day. They have few wants and are temperate. You never see a drunken man in the street. I spent four months in Japan and have visited nearly all of the principal cities. The only intoxicated people I saw were a party of young fellows dressed in fantastic costumes who were sailing down the river in Osaka. The city had been given over to great ceremonies and rejoicings over the return of the soldiers it sent to the war, and these young bloods—five or six of them—were continuing their celebration another day.

This sobriety is due to the use of tea instead of liquor as a beverage. The tea houses in Japan take the place of saloons and they are about as numerous in the large cities as bar-rooms are in Chicago. But a pot of tea that will entertain an entire family can be bought for 2 sen (1 cent in our money), which cheers and

The Yankees of the East

stimulates quite as much as malt or alcoholic liquors. The use of beer is, however, increasing so rapidly in Japan as to excite apprehension, and the government is making it the subject of an inquiry. There is a brewery or two in nearly every city of size and beer can be bought at almost every tea house.

While Mr. Dun does not advise any one to invest money in Japan or enter into mercantile or mechanical affairs there, he recommends those who are looking that way to make a careful personal investigation and consult with Americans of experience. No concessions are necessary, and foreigners are allowed to interest themselves in any enterprise except mining, although until the new treaty goes into effect in 1899 they must confine themselves to the treaty ports and the limits of consular jurisdiction.

The new treaty, which was negotiated by Secretary Gresham and Minister Kurino, in 1894, at Washington, makes Japan as free for foreigners as the United States, with the exception that they cannot own real estate, and by a straight reading of the text it would seem that that is not prohibited. It provides that foreigners may trade by wholesale or retail, singly or with native partners, and says that they "may own, hire and occupy houses, manufactories, warehouses, shops and premises, and lease land" conforming of course to the laws and police

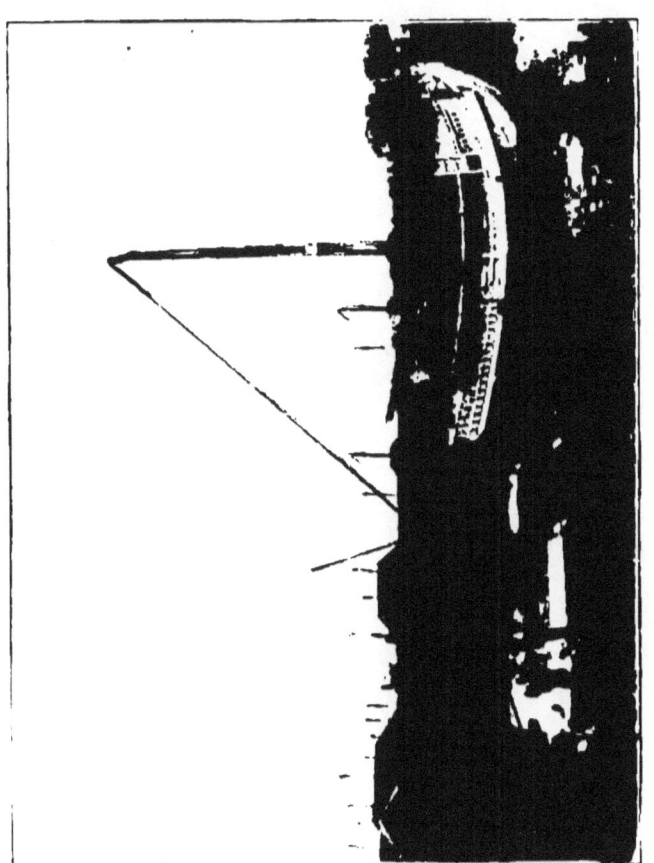

A JAPANESE JUNK.

Concerning Trade and Investments

regulations that apply to them and the natives of the country alike.

If this does not mean that they may both own and lease real estate the English language has lost its significance, but Minister Dun says the treaty is intended to permit people to own buildings but not the land they stand upon.

The treaty also provides that foreigners shall enjoy all rights and privileges enjoyed by natives "in whatever relates to residence and travel, to the possession of goods and effects, to the succession to personal estate and the disposition of property;" that they shall not be required to pay any higher taxes, imposts or charges than natives; that they may freely enjoy their own religion, bury their dead according to their own rites, and that they shall be exempted from military service, forced loans and all other exactions. No higher duties are to be imposed upon the products of the United States than upon those of the most favored nation, and there must be perfect equality in the treatment of Americans and natives in the exportation of merchandise. The coasting trade, as is customary in all countries, is withheld for the benefit of the citizens of Japan, but American vessels laden with cargoes for more than one port are allowed to load and unload wherever they like. The same protection is afforded to natives and foreigners in patents and trademarks, which is a very good

The Yankees of the East

thing, because at present there is no patent treaty between the two countries and the Japanese are stealing all of our inventions.

The foreign settlements which are now subject to the jurisdiction of the consuls of the different countries are to be incorporated into the municipalities which they adjoin, and the consuls will yield control to the local officials.

Until now Japan, like China, Turkey, Egypt and other countries which have not reached a high degree of cilization, has been subjected to what is called the doctrine of extra terrritoriality. That means that the citizens of the United States or England or any other civilized nation residing in those countries are subject to their own laws, administered by their consuls and not to the local authorities or courts. If an American commits a crime in Japan to-day he is tried before the United States consul-general, according to the laws of the United States, and not by the courts and laws of Japan. The same is true of citizens of European nations. If a Japanese citizen commits a crime against an American he is tried by the local authorities. The general rule in civil as well as criminal cases is that the defendant shall be tried under the laws of his own country, and the plaintiff brings his suit accordingly.

But Japan thinks she is sufficiently civilized to administer justice to foreigners and has long

Concerning Trade and Investments

demanded release from the extra territoriality restriction. That release is given her in the treaties that were made with England and the United States last year and recently with Russia, but it does not go into effect for five years from date—that is, July 17, 1899. By that time it is believed that all doubt on the subject of Japanese justice will be removed. But this is a serious question for foreigners, and for those who intend to enter business or invest money in Japan.

As a consolation to those American residents who objected to being placed under the jurisdiction of the Japanese authorities and courts, the treaty was amended in the United States Senate so that it might be terminated upon notice at the end of one year if it was found to be unsatisfactory. In other words, if American residents in Japan became convinced by a year's experience that they could not secure proper protection for their persons and property from the local authorities and justice in the local courts, they would be able upon the demand of our government to return again to the protection of the American consul. But Minister Dun has discovered that by somebody's blunder this provision was so drawn as to prevent the termination of the treaty within less than thirteen years. The language is as follows:

"This treaty shall go into operation on the 17th

The Yankees of the East

day of July, 1899, and shall remain in force for a period of twelve years from that date.

"Either high contracting party shall have the right *at any time thereafter* to give notice to the other of its intention to terminate the same, and, at the expiration of twelve months after such notice is given, the treaty shall wholly cease and terminate."

This discovery caused a profound sensation among the American residents, but Minister Dun does not think there is any occasion for alarm. On the contrary, the officials of the Japanese foreign office have given him cordial and voluntary assurances of their willingness to construe this provision as it was intended and not as it reads.

A majority of the American and British residents were opposed to the ratification of the treaties, and they sent many remonstrances to their governments. They have not sufficient confidence in Japanese justice to submit their persons and properties to the protection of the laws of this country. They prefer to remain under the jurisdiction of their consuls, but you will find a great many of the opposite opinion, who believe that the Japanese laws are liberal and their judges are just. There is plenty of time for improvement, and before the treaty goes into effect in 1899 Japan will have made great progress in this as well as other directions. While one may sympathize with the preference of the foreigners here to live under the laws of

Concerning Trade and Investments

their own countries, it is nevertheless the impression of disinterested observers that life and property are quite as safe in Japan as in Spain, or Italy, or any of the Latin-American republics. There have been a few cases of injustice which are cited whenever this question is discussed—cases in which foreigners have suffered injustice in the courts of Japan when they have been trying to defend their rights or collect dues from the government or Japanese citizens, but the wonder is that such instances are so few. Ten times as many quite as serious might be cited in which the United States government has been the defendant, and which could never have occurred in Japan without an international eruption. No foreigner has ever been treated by the parliament or the people of Japan as badly as Ericsson was treated by the government of the United States, and I might mention other similar historical examples.

There are about 3,000 foreigners in Japan, not including Chinese. The majority of them are Englishmen; Germans are next in number. The Americans constitute perhaps 15 per cent. of the whole. The native population by the census of 1892 was 41,089,940, and for the benefit of the 3,000 foreigners they have been kept in what is practically a commercial bondage since 1858, because in her treaties made at the opening of Japan to foreign settlement the

The Yankees of the East

great nations of the earth allowed her no more authority over her own tariff than over the stranger within her gates. She cannot impose a higher duty than 5 per cent. on any foreign merchandise, and must tax her farmers to pay the expenses of her government, including the best lighthouse system in the world.

Japan is the only country that does not tax foreign ships for lighthouse, harbor or tonnage dues, and every foreigner in Japan, no matter what amount of property he may own or what business he may be engaged in, is entirely exempt from all taxation. The government furnishes him police protection; he has the benefit of a paid fire department, and in most of the cities water and sewerage systems, but he is not required to contribute anything to their support.

Japan has thought for many years that she has reached a stage of civilization that should justify her in assuming authority over all the inhabitants of this empire, and the treaties made in 1894 agree that she may do so at the end of this century. Then any foreigner may enter into any lawful enterprise as freely as any citizen, but until that date it will be necessary for foreigners to confine their manufacturing and commercial establishments to the limits of the consular jurisdiction or entrust their interests to the care of native banks in the capacity of trustees.

Concerning Trade and Investments

There are one hundred and eighty-four foreign firms doing business in Yokohama; sixty-five are English, thirty-five American, twenty-nine German, twenty French, twelve Swiss. The remainder are Italians, Hindoos, Chinese, Austrians and Russians. While the Englishmen command the largest amount of capital, and consequently the larger proportion of the trade, there are no men in that colony, or in any other foreign colony throughout the world, for that matter, who are better representatives of American enterprise and manhood than Mr. James R. Morse, president of the American Trading company; Mr. B. C. Howard, general manager of the Pacific Mail steamship line; Mr. George Middleton of Middleton & Co., Mr. Julius W. Copmann of the Standard Oil company and others who might be mentioned with them. Their wives are fit examples of American womanhood and their homes of American homes.

It is unfortunate that in Japan, as elsewhere over the world, with the exception of some of the larger cities of Europe, there is no American banking house, and our people have to do their business through London, Banking pays better than it does in Europe or America, and the business is expanding every year. The increase within the next four or five years will be greater than it has ever been, and no better opportunity

The Yankees of the East

is offered anywhere for the right kind of men with an adequate amount of capital.

A firm, or company, or individual, before it can commence business, must register with the proper authorities its title and a copy of the stamp or seal used instead of a signature; there must also be a description of the nature of the business, together with a detailed account of the capital, securities, and other financial details. The books kept by the firm are considered private property, but in certain cases a court of law may require their production, or may appoint an official to examine them. A house may be registered in three ways: First, as a Gomeikwaisha, or private firm. In this case, the firm always goes by a family name, and the business is looked upon strictly as a family concern. In such cases the government interferes very little with its affairs, and the firm is left practically unfettered in the details of its business. But if a private firm of this kind be desirous of extending its business by inviting the assistance of capital outside of the family, it may, in Japanese law, take a position half way between a private firm and a joint-stock company. This is known as a Goshikwaisha. The law provides for the protection of the capital thus invited into the firm. The partners in the old firm still retain a principal interest in the business, but they are subject to the control of the shareholders.

Concerning Trade and Investments

Shares in a Goshikwaisha can only be bought and sold with the sanction of the other shareholders. This institution is peculiar to Japan.

Kabushikiwaisha, or joint-stock companies, differ from the Goshikwaisha in the fact that their officers are elective at a general meeting of shareholders, and the shares may be bought or sold without the sanction of the other members. These companies are also far more open to government interference. The Department of Commerce and Agriculture, which has cognizance of mercantile affairs, can order an investigation of the affairs of a company at any time, of its own motion; and the district court can, on the requisition of shareholders representing one-fifth of the capital, order a similar inquiry. The officials thus appointed by the ministry or local court have very full powers of inspection and investigation.

Two codes of commercial law have been in use since the reformation. The first was compiled by an American professor in the university and was based entirely upon European precedents. It met with such opposition from the merchants and bankers that much of it had to be withdrawn and a new code was prepared by a commission which is still in session revising the other laws of the country. The most important title in the commercial code is that relating to bankruptcy.

The Yankees of the East

When proceedings in bankruptcy have been instituted against a debtor the court appoints an assignee who has authority to act until the whole business is settled according to the requirements of the law. When once the assignee has been appointed the debtor loses a large degree of his personal liberty. He cannot change his residence without the permission of the court; he is obliged to appear whenever required; he may be placed under surveillance, and required to give bail, failing which he may be kept in detention. He is incapable of all commercial transactions; cannot hold any office of trust or emolument in any business house or company; he cannot alienate his personal property; even his correspondence and telegrams may be opened and read by the assignee. The debtor may, however, postpone bankruptcy proceedings by obtaining a shiharai yuo (decree of postponement); but in this case he must be able to show that his difficulties are only temporary, and that, with time, he can succeed in extricating himself. The assignee may sell all the property owned by the bankrupt, real and personal, at auction or otherwise, collect all his bills payable for their full amount or by compromise, and divide the proceeds among the creditors, pro rata, subject to the approval of the court.

The postal savings bank has been a great success in Japan, and is found to be a most use-

Concerning Trade and Investments

ful and convenient method of encouraging economy among the laboring classes. In 1893 there were 989,092 depositors out of a total of forty-one million population; in 1894 the number increased to 1,076,000, and in 1895, 1,139,-331. The amount of the deposits in 1893 were $24,586,586; in 1894, $26,082,789, and in 1895, $26,646,102.

Mr. Yesabro Wooyeno of the Kansai Trading company of Kyoto and New York city is one of the largest native dealers in miscellaneous American merchandise in the empire. He does both an exporting and importing business, dividing his time between the two countries, and his experience qualifies him to speak intelligently of the condition and obstacles of trade. Mr. Wooyeno kindly explained to me the difficulties he had met with in his endeavors to extend the market for American manufactured articles in Japan. He said there was no question as to the superiority of a large class of our goods. The French made better gloves, ribbons, toys and fancy articles, and in some products the English manufacturers surpassed those of the United States, but the people of Japan have learned by experience that any article manufactured in the latter country is of a higher grade in quality than can be found elsewhere, and are usually willing to pay a little more for it on that account. There is not so great a difference in prices, how-

The Yankees of the East

ever, as people generally suppose, and that would not be a serious obstacle were freights from New York and interior points in the United States as low as those from Europe. That, Mr. Wooyeno said, was the serious feature of the commercial problem, and while the market for manufactured goods in Japan was already limited, and would be growing smaller every year, there was and would be a steady demand for foreign machinery which might be supplied from the United States if transportation charges were anywhere near as low as from Europe.

The market in Japan for raw materials, principally cotton and iron, was very large, and would soon be enormous, but strange to say, it is the habit of Japanese factory managers to buy raw material in Liverpool and London than in the United States. Mr. Wooyeno cannot explain why, but American cotton can be purchased and shipped from Liverpool to Osaka for several cents a pound less than from any port in the United States, and pay a profit to the British middlemen at the same time. The difference is sufficient to represent a considerable dividend in a year's business. For example, the rate on baled cotton from St. Louis to Osaka by the Northern Pacific Railway and Steamship line is $24 a ton, and by the Pacific Mail $28 a ton, whether it goes by railway overland or from New Orleans via Panama up the Pacific coast to

Concerning Trade and Investments

San Francisco: while the rate from London to Osaka is only about $10 a ton on the regular lines of steamers and much less than that by tramps. An immense amount of cotton is shipped from the Atlantic ports of the United States to Japan by way of Liverpool and London which never leaves the steamer. It is originally billed to British ports and there resold to the agents of the Osaka mills.

Mr. Wooyeno does not know of any attempt to sell direct from the United States to the Osaka manufacturers, although he thinks it would be a very profitable business. And there does not seem to be any reason why cotton may not be shipped by steamers, or sailing vessels, from the Atlantic and gulf ports of the United States, just as kerosene oil is sent from New York and Philadelphia. The Standard Oil company has a regular line of iron sailing vessels, carrying 3,000 and 4,000 tons each, which are dispatched at frequent intervals for the Japanese and Chinese ports, and bring back tea, silk and rice as a return cargo. The charter rates for such vessels for either cotton or iron would be from $4 to $6 a ton, and the difference between those rates and the steamship charges would make a man rich very soon.

Nobody knows why this has not been done. It is a commercial phenomenon that our cotton factors have not attempted a direct trade with

The Yankees of the East

consumers in Japan. The shipment of miscellaneous goods by sailing vessels is a different matter, for unless a man has a full cargo and can charter a vessel he is subject to great delay and inconvenience. He has to wait until a ship is coming his way, or find some one else to join him in the charter.

It is easier to ship goods to China by sailing vessels than to Japan, because there is a steady demand for American shirtings, sheetings and drillings in the former country, and the New York agents and the New England mills are almost always willing to furnish a part of a cargo.

The average rate of freight on general merchandise from New York and Philadelphia to Yokohama by sea and rail via San Francisco, Tacoma or Vancouver is from $35 to $50 a ton, and by Panama from $30 to $40 a ton. The transportation companies reserve the option to charge by weight or measurement, whichever amounts to the most. On heavy machinery they charge by weight. On light goods in wooden cases they charge by measurement, forty cubic feet to a ton—that is, a package about three and a half feet square.

The same goods may be shipped from England for from thirty-five to fifty shillings or about one-fourth the charges from the United States on the regular steamers, and for even less

Concerning Trade and Investments

by tramps that come over here for silk and tea. From Hamburg the rates are about the same, and from Marseilles they are less.

There are often tramp steamers at New York loading for Japan, which carry heavy machinery for $8, $10 and $15 a ton, according to the class of goods and the demand. The lowest rate of freight Mr. Wooyeno ever paid from New York was nineteen shillings on a sailing vessel. His goods were six months in coming, but arrived in excellent order.

The freights from Japan to the United States are much more reasonable. By San Francisco they were formerly $14 and $16 a ton on general merchandise, but since the Northern Pacific and the Oregon Railway and Navigation company put on steamers they have been reduced to $11. The rates to London on the same classes of goods are from thirty to forty shillings, or from $8 to $10 a ton; to Hamburg they are about the same and to Marseilles forty francs. Tramps and sailing vessels that take out oil will accept cargoes to New York at very low prices, often $5 and $6 a ton.

The rate on raw silk to New York, London, Marseilles and Hamburg is about the same on all the regular steamship lines, usually $4 per hundredweight. On tramp steamers and sailing vessels it is much cheaper. Silk goods by San Francisco or Vancouver to Chicago and New

The Yankees of the East

York are charged $2.50 per hundredweight, and one per cent of their value. The rate to London by sea is one and one-fourth per cent of their value and to Marseilles about the same. The rate on tea to New York and Chicago via San Francisco and Vancouver is $8 per ton of forty cubic feet. A great deal is carried by tramps and sailing vessels, which usually charge three-fourths of a cent per pound. The rate to London is fifty shillings a ton and to Marseilles fifty francs.

Mr. Wooyeno imports a great deal of tobacco leaf and cigarettes from the United States, and the demand is increasing every year. He also imports lead pencils, celluloid articles and novelties of all kinds.

"A great many more manufactured goods might be sold in Japan," said Mr. Wooyeno, "if the manufacturers would study the market carefully and make modifications in them to comply with the peculiarities of the people. I tried to introduce stoves into Japan, both for coal and oil, but they are not popular. The people prefer charcoal. I have also failed to sell cotton and woolen goods and hats and caps. The American articles are of finer quality, but the French and English seem to suit the taste of the people better and sell their goods cheaper. I have sold a good deal of railway material, but five or six years ago the government adopted the

Concerning Trade and Investments

English system of railways and has since bought all its supplies in Great Britain. Some of the private companies purchased locomotives from the Baldwin company of Philadelphia, but they are now making their own on the Baldwin patents. The material comes from England and some of the finer parts from the United States. In the course of a few years Japan will supply herself with all the railway material needed.

"Yes, there are plenty of profitable opportunities for Americans to enter into manufacturing enterprises in Japan," said Mr. Wooyeno. "Our labor is good and cheap, but we must have foreign superintendents. When a manager has been educated abroad he does very well, but men of home education require a long time to fit themselves to superintend mechanical apparatus, and before Japan can become a manufacturing nation we must not only have foreign machinery, but foreigners to superintend its operation and to teach our operatives.

"American capital, if wisely invested here, is just as safe as in the United States, and will pay much larger dividends. The investors, however, should be very careful whom they enter into partnership with, for we have our share of rascals, and they are always on the lookout for victims. It is only necessary to operate through well-established banks and other reputable agencies. The average of commercial honesty is as

The Yankees of the East

high in Japan as it is anywhere else in the world, but when a foreigner is swindled he makes such a fuss about it that the facts are always well advertised. A great many men come here from foreign countries expecting to get rich rapidly by speculative transactions. They take large risks and they engage with unreliable men, and as a natural consequence they lose their money. Then they go home and blame the entire population of Japan for their misfortune.

"The great difficulty in manufacturing silk piece goods in Japan," said Mr. Wooyeno, "is that the fashions change so often. The French manufacturers set the styles, and it takes a long time to get the Japanese weavers, who generally work in their own households, to adopt them. They are very slow and conservative, and when they set their looms for a certain pattern they don't want to change them. The only way to remedy this is to establish silk factories under the direction of foreign superintendents with modern looms.

"No, I do not think there would be any trouble with the guilds, although the workingmen of Japan are sure to organize for self-protection and to promote their mutual welfare. When they are thoroughly trained to handle modern machinery they will naturally demand advanced pay, but labor is so abundant here and the cost of living so small, that wages will never

Concerning Trade and Investments

be as high as they are in the United States or Europe.

"Yes, the working people are gradually getting modern ideas through the newspapers, and agitators are beginning to appear among them from the soshi class, who are drifting toward socialism. The honest, industrious laborers have always had a contempt for the soshi, because they are idle, worthless vagabonds. Thus far their influence has been very small, and there is nothing to fear from them at present, but whenever any labor trouble or dissatisfaction occurs they are likely to interfere and increase it.

"No, I do not think the industrial arts of Japan are in a state of decay. The artists now living are doing just as good work as was ever done, but less of it. The demand for first-class cloisenne, ceramics and bronze work is limited, while the market for the cheaper qualities is large and profitable. It is, therefore, perfectly natural that the artists should take advantage of that fact and produce the kind of goods that will bring them money instead of great reputation. But we have many men in Japan to-day who can produce as fine work as was ever created, if any one will give them an order."

A great deal of commotion was excited in commercial circles in the summer of 1895 by an incident of dishonest dealing that will furnish the critics of Japan with another illustration to

The Yankees of the East

point their morals and adorn their tales. It is very unfortunate that it should happen just when an effort was being made to build up a foreign trade and to make a series of treaties with the European powers, under which Japan shall be recognized as a fully civilized country, capable of conducting her international relations according to the highest standard of morality and administering impartial justice in her courts. It is fortunate at the same time that the Japanese judges in this particular instance demonstrated that they can do justice even in disputes between foreigners and their fellow-citizens, but the record of the native merchants for commercial integrity has received a dark blot that will require many years to efface.

Mr. Kimura, one of the wealthiest men in Japan, a large manufacturer, the managing director of the Specie Bank, one of the largest and best managed financial institutions in the country, and interested in other extensive enterprises, made a contract to purchase 100 bales of yarn from Cornes & Co., an English firm, at a certain price. Before the goods arrived from England the price fell, and the purchaser declined to accept them when offered, pleading a technicality. Cornes & Co. parleyed awhile and then went into court, where judgment was rendered for the plaintiff, requiring the defendant to accept the 100 bales and pay the full

Concerning Trade and Investments

price for them, with insurance and warehouse charges and interest to date of delivery. It was plain to the court, as it was to everybody else familiar with the facts, that Mr. Kimura wanted to get out of a bad bargain, and that his technical objections to accepting the goods were invented for that purpose. For that reason the court threw out a lot of testimony offered by the defendant to sustain his position. Justice is swift and sure in Japan, and the courts apply the rules of common sense more generally than what we call the rules of evidence.

Although the court decided against him, Mr. Kimura still declined to pay for the goods, and sent a committee from the guild of yarn and woven goods dealers to Messrs. Cornes & Co., offering to take one-half of the invoice and divide with them the losses that were occasioned by the reduction in the price of yarn. Cornes & Co. declined to accept any such compromise or to consider any proposition beyond the strict fulfillment of the contract, whereupon the committee from the guild notified them that if they insisted upon the enforcement of the judgment of the court they might expect no further business with native dealers in yarns and woven goods. In other words, a boycott was declared.

This got into the newspapers and created a great deal of controversy and excitement in commercial circles, for, as one newspaper ex-

The Yankees of the East

pressed it, if foreign merchants are to be boycotted because they insist upon native merchants carrying out their contracts the new treaties might as well be cancelled and all the foreign merchants had better close their doors. Many of the native newspapers attacked Kimura and the yarn dealers' guild savagely, and declared that they were unfit representatives of the commercial classes of Japan, and most of the press, to the credit of the country, condemned the proceedings as dishonorable and called upon parliament to enact a law prohibiting the despicable expedient of boycotting.

Through official influence, and perhaps because the yarn-dealers found public opinion was so generally against them, the guild negotiated a compromise under which Mr. Kimura agreed to take the yarn at the original contract price, and Cornes & Co. agreed to pay the cost of the litigation, the warehouse fees, insurance and other charges. The boycott was declared off, but it will be a long time before the people of Japan hear the last of it.

A prominent official of the government, while lamenting the dishonorable attempt of so promit anen man as Mr. Kimura to shoulder his losses in an ordinary commercial transaction upon a foreigner, because of the injury to the credit of the country, at the same time insisted that he was simply repeating an old trick that

Concerning Trade and Investments

had been played upon the Japanese by Englishmen a great many times.

"When foreigners first came into this country to do business," said he, "such things were of frequent occurrence, and the Japanese were always the victims. The English were often dishonorable in their commercial transactions, and arbitrary and overbearing in their manners. When they found themselves on the wrong side of a bargain they would usually refuse to carry it out, and were always backed up by Sir Harry Parkes, the British minister, and a fleet of gunboats. Sir Harry was the most vigorous and conspicuous foreigner in the east in those days and served as her majesty's minister both in China and Japan. He was what you call a bulldozer; he was always on the side of the Englishman, right or wrong, and always insisted upon having things his own way, in which he usually succeeded, because his government kept a big fleet of gunboats to emphasize his views. I suppose there were hundreds of cases similar to that of Kimura vs. Cornes, and they were all decided in favor of the Englishmen. Other nationalities had occasional disputes, but the British had the most of them."

"This led to a very bitter feeling between foreign and native merchants, which still exists to a considerable degree, although it has been greatly modified. As a rule the foreign merchants stand together when one of their number has trouble, and the yarn-dealers' guild was simply following their example. Mind you, I do not justify it in the slightest degree. I am only giving you the reasons why the present unfortunate case occurred, and I am glad that public opinion and the newspapers have demonstrated that such transactions are not popular in Japan."

About the same time we had a forcible demonstration of the causes why the United States has so small a share of the import trade of Japan. During the last ten years we have purchased from Japan raw material to the value of 264,417,237 yen, and have sold her merchandise to the value of 57,960,908 yen. At the same time Great Britain has sold Japan merchandise to the value of 236,415,892 yen, and has purchased of her only 52,641,903 yen worth of her products. A yen is worth about half a dollar. The reason of this is that Englishmen are willing to meet the requirements of the market, and observe the arbitrary conditions of the trade, while our people insist that the Japanese shall adopt our methods and accept our conditions. In other words, the Europeans have been willing to do business upon the terms of the Japanese, while the Americans have insisted upon fixing the terms to suit themselves.

Here is an illustration of what has happened

Concerning Trade and Investments

continually for years: The city of Tokyo is introducing a modern system of waterworks and will require pumping machinery costing about $1,500,000 and about 50,000 tons of iron pipe, worth about as much more. A company of local capitalists was organized to make the pipe and put up a plant on the banks of the river near Tokyo. The machinery was all first-class, of English manufacture, and about $300,000 was invested. But the pipe they turned out proved to be poor stuff and very expensive. Nearly half of it was condemned as worthless, which made the remainder cost from $50 to $80 a ton, while a much superior quality could be imported for $30. This was due to the poor material used and to the ignorance and inexperience of the managers and the men employed. The machinery was set up and put in operation by a young engineer who graduated from the Troy polytechnic school, but had never worked in a foundry, and the superintendent and his assistants—in fact, all hands about the place—undertook to make pipe as a cook would make a cake from a description of the process they found in a book. Not one of them had ever seen the operation.

The local enterprise having failed, the city authorities called for bids from pipe manufacturers in England, Scotland, France, Germany, Belgium and the United States upon carefully

The Yankees of the East

prepared specifications. Three American firms were asked to submit proposals, but only one in each of the others. One of the firms in our country, a Philadelphia concern, declined to consider the matter at all. Another manufacturer made estimates, but did not submit them, while the third was the lowest bidder and was awarded the contract, but he refused to make a deposit of $40,000, or 10 per cent of the contract, as earnest money, to be forfeited in case of his failure to fulfill the terms. The contract was therefore awarded to an iron company at Liege, Belgium, at a price which gave them an enormous profit compared with what American manufacturers are in the habit of enjoying when they do public work.

The second letting, for 14,000 tons, soon followed. Although the city officials were disgusted at the lack of faith shown by the American firm that was awarded the last contract, they invited the same people to bid again, and the same bidder, an Alabama company, was by far the lowest again, which shows that we can compete in prices with the world. But this proposal was rejected without ceremony or consideration, because it did not comply with the specifications. It stipulated that the pipe should be inspected, delivered and paid for before it left the United States. Another American company requested that the specifications be changed to

Concerning Trade and Investments

read that way, but the city authorities politely declined to make such a concession. They explained that whenever the government of Japan had purchased foreign supplies during the last twenty-five years it had always been upon the same terms and conditions—that is, payment in cash within three days after inspection and delivery in that country, and it could not change its methods without much trouble and expense. If it accepted the pipe in America it would be compelled to send agents and inspectors over there and pay some commission house for looking after the chartering of vessels and attending to the details of shipping.

Both of the American firms invited to submit proposals sent agents to Japan to make inquiries. One of these agents was the vice-president of the company he represented, and he was assisted by a representative of their New York selling agents, who do a large export business. These gentlemen made a thorough investigation and reported strongly in favor of securing the contract if possible on any terms, not only because they believed there was a large profit in it, but also, what was more important, that it would give them an advantage in securing future business in Japan, because other cities are certain to follow the example of Tokyo in establishing water works and other modern improvements.

The American minister, the American con-

The Yankees of the East

sul-general and all the bankers and business men they talked with told them that the city of Tokyo had as good a credit as Boston or Berlin, that there was not the slightest risk of securing payment if the contract was complied with, and that there was a very strong desire on the part of the government to give the business to an American firm. The minister of public works said that preference would be given to American bidders wherever it was possible, and expressed the hope that all three of the firms invited would submit proposals.

But the directors of the two companies at home lacked confidence in the reports of their agents, or for some other reason both declined to comply with the specifications. One of them, as I have said, refused to submit any bid whatever unless the contract could provide for delivery and payment in the United States, but a proposal was submitted in its behalf by a firm of American merchants in Yokohama who assumed all responsibility. The second American firm submitted a bid for delivery at Pensacola, Newport News, or any Atlantic or gulf port, although it was aware of the refusal to change the specifications in this respect.

Its bid was the lowest submitted—nearly twenty per cent lower than any other—but the committee of the common council in charge of

Concerning Trade and Investments

the business threw it out without further examination, and felt that it was a reflection upon their integrity.

A prominent Japanese official commenting upon this remarked that the government had the kindliest feelings toward the United States, and was anxious to do everything in its power to promote trade between the two countries. This sentiment, he said, was thoroughly understood by all Americans who had ever done business in Japan or had even visited that country. Therefore it was exasperating to their self-respect and sense of justice to have two prominent American manufacturers, who were asked to accept this contract, imply by the conditions they exacted that the city of Tokyo might possibly refuse to pay for the pipe after it was delivered. He said there had never been a question or a criticism of the honesty or fairness of Japanese officials in connection with their purchases or their public works, and the manufacturers of America were the only ones who had ever expressed a doubt on that subject.

"Your people can have this contract if they want it," he said, "and it amounts to several hundred thousand dollars. And there are other contracts of the same sort to be let in the future which they can also have. Our people have offered to give them advantages over bidders from every other country, but it is not quite complimentary to our honesty nor is it very encouraging to our efforts to build up a trade with your country to have your manufacturers insinuate that we do not intend to pay for the goods we order."

There were bidders from England, Scotland, Germany, France and Belgium who were willing to accept all conditions and requirements. The Americans were the only ones who suggested any change, and the contract was let to the lowest European bidder—a firm at Glasgow.

Mr. J. R. Morse, a prominent American merchant in Yokohama, was sent to the United States some years ago to secure bids for nearly $1,000,000 worth of steel railway bridges. He was not permitted to close contracts, but was empowered to obtain estimates to be submitted to the Japanese government, which intended to compare them with those from other countries; but Mr. Morse was authorized to promise that American manufacturers would receive the business if their bids were not more than 25 per cent higher than those of England, Germany and Belgium. He visited New York, Philadelphia, Pittsburg, Cleveland, Chicago and other cities, but the only bridge-builders he was able to persuade to offer estimates were at San Francisco, and their prices

Concerning Trade and Investments

were very much higher than the lowest received from Europe.

Several American companies were willing to prepare bids provided Mr. Morse would guarantee them the work. Others refused to do so unless a deposit of money was made to secure them against the loss of their time and trouble. Still more demanded that the specifications and terms of the contract be changed to meet their wishes. In other words they insisted upon furnishing such bridges as they pleased and not such as the Japanese government wanted, and they endeavored to convince Mr. Morse that the Japanese did not know what was good for them. Nearly every firm that was approached on the subject required that the bridges should be inspected, accepted and paid for at the factories in the United States, and not upon delivery in Japan, as the specifications stated. In other words they expressed a doubt of the good faith and responsibility of the Japanese government which was very embarrassing to Mr. Morse when he came to make his report. No such objections were found in Europe. There was not a manufacturer in England, Germany or Belgium that did not jump at the contract, and it was finally let to a British company.

The American merchants in Yokohama say that this is not an unusual experience. Similar

The Yankees of the East

cases are occurring all the time. It is the invariable habit of the American manufacturer who is offered business in Japan to imply, if he does not express, a doubt of the integrity of the government or the people, but the Europeans are never afraid to accept any business they can get, and at very small margins.

PRINTED BY JOHN WILSON AND SON AT
THE UNIVERSITY PRESS IN CAMBRIDGE
DURING JUNE M DCCC XCVI. FOR
STONE AND KIMBALL
NEW YORK

www.ingramcontent.com/pod-product-compliance
Lightning Source LLC
Chambersburg PA
CBHW030407230426
43664CB00007BB/779